HC

α

OXFORD CHILDREN'S

Spanish · English

Visual DICTIONARY

OXFORD
UNIVERSITY PRESS

Índice de contenido

Cómo utilizar este diccinario • *How to use this dictionary*   **6-7**
Apoyo lingüístico • *Language support*   **8-9**

Gente y hogares • *People and homes*

La familia y los amigos • *Family and friends*   **10-11**
Tu cuerpo • *Your body*   **12-13**
En tu cuerpo • *Inside your body*   **14-15**
Los sentidos y los sentimientos • *Senses and feelings*   **16-17**
La casa • *Home*   **18-19**
Los artículos de la casa • *Household objects*   **20-21**

Alimentos y ropa • *Food and clothing*

Comida y bebidas • *Food and drink*   **22-23**
Todo tipo de comida • *All sorts of food*   **24-25**
Frutas y verduras • *Fruit and vegetables*   **26-27**
Ropa de diario • *Everyday clothes*   **28-29**
Todo tipo de ropa • *All sorts of clothes*   **30-31**

Colegio y trabajo • *School and work*

En la escuela • *At school*   **32-33**
Todo tipo de trabajos • *All sorts of work*   **34-35**
Equipo y ropa de trabajo • *Work equipment and clothing*   **36-37**

Deportes y ocio • *Sport and leisure*

Deporte • *Sports*   **38-39**
Deporte en acción • *Sports in action*   **40-41**
Juegos y pasatiempos • *Games and leisure*   **42-43**

Artes plásticas, música y espectáculos • *Art, music, and entertainment*

Artes plásticas y manualidades • *Art*   **44-45**
Instrumentos musicales • *Musical instruments*   **46-47**
Música y baile • *Music and dance*   **48-49**
Televisión, cine y teatro • *TV, film, and theatre*   **50-51**
Programas de televisión y películas • *TV shows and films*   **52-53**

Viajes y medios de transporte • *Travel and transport*

Vehículos de pasajeros • *Passenger vehicles*   **54-55**
Vehículos pesados • *Working vehicles*   **56-57**
Aeronaves • *Aircraft*   **58-59**
Buques, barcos y otras embarcaciones • *Ships, boats, and other craft*   **60-61**

Contents

Ciencia y tecnología • *Science and technology*

Energía • *Energy and power*	**62-63**
Todo tipo de materiales • *All kinds of materials*	**64-65**
Edificios y estructuras • *Buildings and structures*	**66-67**
Fuerzas y máquinas • *Forces and machines*	**68-69**
Ordenadores y dispositivos electrónicos • *Computers and electronic devices*	**70-71**

Animales y plantas • *Animals and plants*

Mamíferos • *Mammals*	**72-73**
Animales domésticos • *Working animals*	**74-75**
Reptiles y anfibios • *Reptiles and amphibians*	**76-77**
Peces • *Fish*	**78-79**
Animales marinos • *Sea creatures*	**80-81**
Insectos y bichos • *Insects and mini-beasts*	**82-83**
Animales nocturnos • *Nocturnal creatures*	**84-85**
Aves • *Birds*	**86-87**
Árboles y arbustos • *Trees and shrubs*	**88-89**
Todo tipo de plantas • *All sorts of plants*	**90-91**

La Tierra y el medio ambiente • *Planet Earth and the environment*

Pueblos y ciudades • *Towns and cities*	**92-93**
En la calle • *On the street*	**94-95**
En el campo • *In the country*	**96-97**
Paisajes y hábitats • *Landscapes and habitats*	**98-99**
El tiempo • *The weather*	**100-101**
Contaminación y conservación • *Pollution and conservation*	**102-103**
La Tierra • *Planet Earth*	**104-105**

El espacio y los viajes espaciales • *Space and space travel*

El sistema solar • *The solar system*	**106-107**
Viajes espaciales • *Space travel*	**108-109**

Los números y las unidades de medidas • *Counting, numbers, and measurements*	**110-111**
El calendario y la hora • *Calendar and time*	**112-113**
Los colores y las formas • *Colours and shapes*	**114**
Opuestos y palabras de posición • *Opposites and position words*	**115**

Índice español • *Spanish index*	**116-121**
Índice inglés • *English index*	**122-127**

Cómo utilizar este diccinario

Este diccionario está lleno de palabras útiles, y es también un libro informativo. Te ayudará a descubrir más cosas sobre el mundo y a la vez aprenderás palabras nuevas en los dos idiomas.

This dictionary is packed with useful words, and it is also an information book. It will help you find out more about the world at the same time as you are learning new words in two languages.

¿Cómo está organizado? • *How is it organized?*

El diccionario se divide en 10 temas, incluyendo Gente y hogares, Colegio y trabajo, Animales y plantas, Ciencia y tecnología, y muchos más. Cada tema dedica varias páginas a diferentes aspectos del mismo, como La familia y los amigos, Tu cuerpo y Los sentidos y las emociones.

The dictionary is divided into 10 topics, including People and homes, School and work, Animals and plants, and Science and technology. Within each topic there are pages on different subjects, such as Family and friends, Your body, and Senses and feelings.

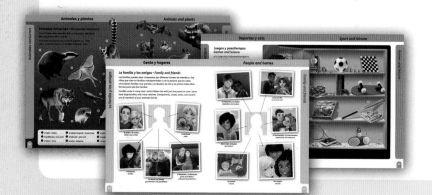

Puedes buscar un tema en el que estés especialmente interesado y leerlo hasta el final, o puedes buscar en el diccionario.

You can find a topic that specially interests you and work right through it. Or you can dip into the dictionary wherever you want.

¿Cómo buscar una palabra? • *How do I find a word?*

Hay dos formas de buscar una palabra.
There are two ways to search for a word.

Puedes buscar los temas en la página del Índice de contenido.

You can look through the topics on the CONTENTS PAGE.

Índice de

Cómo utilizar este diccionario • *How to use this dictiona*
Apoyo lingüístico • *Language support*

Gente y hogares • *People and homes*
La familia y los amigos • *Family and friends*
Tu cuerpo • *Your body*
En tu cuerpo • *Inside your body*
Los sentidos y los sentimientos • *Senses and feelir*
La casa • *Home*
Los artículos de la casa • *Household objects*

Alimentos y ropa • *Food and clothi*
Comida y bebidas • *Food and dri*
 ·do tipo de comida • *Al*

Cada tema utiliza un código de colores.

Each topic is colour-coded.

How to use this dictionary

Cómo utilizar el diccionario • *Using the dictionary*

En cada página, se introducen las palabras utilizando ilustraciones, escenas, y diagramas con etiquetas. Así es fácil encontrar la palabra que se busca, y al mismo tiempo descubrir muchas más.

On each page, words are introduced through lively images, scenes, and labelled diagrams. So it's easy to find the word you need – and discover many more words along the way.

Los recuadros ofrecen vocabulario más completo.

Feature panels give more in-depth vocabulary.

La barra lateral identifica la materia a tratar.

Side bar identifies the subject.

La introducción en los dos idiomas da información adicional sobre el tema.

Introduction in both languages adds extra information on the subject.

La barra superior identifica el tema.

Top bar identifies the topic section.

El texto de las ilustraciones está en los dos idiomas.

Captions provide words or phrases in two languages.

Las etiquetas ayudan a precisar el significado exacto de una palabra.

Labels help to pinpoint the exact meaning of a word.

O puedes consultar el índice del final del libro.

*Or you can use the **INDEX** at the back of the book.*

Hay un Índice inglés y otro español, así que puedes buscar las palabras en cualquiera de los dos idiomas.

There is an English and a Spanish index, so you can find a word in either language.

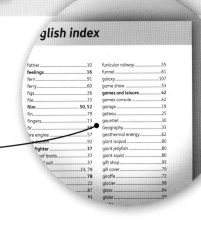

English index	
father	10
feelings	**16**
fern	91
ferry	60
figs	26
file	33
film	**50, 52**
fin	79
fingers	13
fir	89
fire engine	57
season	92
fighter	**37**
of boots	37
f suit	37
	23, 78
	78
	22
	87
	83
funicular railway	55
funnel	61
galaxy	107
game show	53
games and leisure	**42**
games console	42
garage	19
gateau	25
gauntlet	30
Geography	33
geothermal energy	62
giant isopod	80
giant jellyfish	80
giant squid	80
gift shop	95
gill cover	79
giraffe	72
glacier	98
glass	64
glider	59

Sea como sea, te resultará divertido explorar las lustraciones y las palabras.

However you find your word, you will have fun exploring pictures and words!

This book is for people learning their first words in Spanish. By looking at the pictures you can learn the words for a whole range of themes.

Most of the words in this book are nouns, but some are verbs and some are adjectives. Nouns are words that give names to things, people or places. For example, **cuchara** (spoon), **padre** (father), and **bota** (boot) are all nouns. Verbs are doing words; they refer to actions. For example, **golpear** (hit), **tirar** (throw), and **patinar** (skate) are all verbs.

Most nouns are either masculine or feminine in Spanish. We call this gender, and this is shown in this book by putting the word for 'the' before the noun: **el** (masculine) or **la** (feminine).

Most nouns ending in 'o' are masculine, for example **el hermano** (brother), **el brazo** (arm), **el cuchillo** (knife) . Most ending in 'a' are feminine, such as **la hermana** (sister), **la oreja** (ear), **la cuchara** (spoon). But take care! Some words ending in 'a' are masculine, such as **el mapa** (map), **el problema** (problem) and **el planeta** (planet). Similarly, a few words ending in 'o' are feminine: **la mano** (hand).

TIP: When you learn a new word, always try to learn whether it is masculine or feminine.

We say that a noun is 'plural' when it refers to two or more things. You make the plural of Spanish nouns ending in 'o' or 'a' by adding an 's': **hermanos, orejas**. When a word ends with a consonant, the plural is –es: **conductores, pasteles** .

The word for 'the' with plural masculine nouns is los; with plural feminine nouns, use **las: los desiertos, las montañas.**

Adjectives are words that describe nouns; for example, **grande** (big), **pequeño** (small). Many adjectives have a different form for masculine and feminine: often you just change the final 'o' to 'a' to make the feminine adjective from the masculine form; **el castillo alto, la torre alta.** On the other hand, many adjectives are the same for masculine and feminine, as with these hot drinks: **el chocolate caliente, el café caliente.**

It's the same with job titles: as in English, some jobs have different forms depending on whether you're talking about a man or a woman: **el actor, la actriz** – but with others, only the word for 'the' changes: you'd say **la dentista** for a female dentist, but **el dentista** for a male dentist.

Pronunciation

Working out how to say Spanish words is logical once you know the basic sounds. Here's a pronunciation guide for single letters and groups of letters.

Single letters

b –*corbata, abogado, balón.* **'b' and 'v' sound the same.**

c (+a, o, u): – 'k': *campo, cocodrilo, cuchillo*

c (+e, i) – 'th' in most of Spain: 's' in most of Latin America: *baloncesto, cinturón*

cc (k-th): *fricción, ciencia ficción*

d: sounds like the English 'd' at the start of a word, e.g. *dibujo.* **But it sounds like 'th' in 'that' in other parts of the word:** *nadar, Madrid.*

g (+ a, o, u): like 'g' in 'gun': *galleta, algodón, hamburguesa*

g (+e, i) – like 'ch' in the Scottish 'loch': *ligero, rígido*

j – like 'ch' in the Scottish 'loch': *ojo, traje, juego*

n – like the English 'n': *nariz, ensalada.*

ñ – 'ny', like in 'onion': *muñeca, albañil*

r – quickly roll your tongue on the roof of your mouth – *historia, rueda.*
Make a longer roll for the double 'r': *gorro*

u – on it own, it sounds like 'oo' in 'look': *duro;* **it sounds the English 'w' when it follows another vowel:** *bueno.* **In some groups of letters, the 'u' is silent: 'gue'** *(hamburguesa),* **'gui'** *(guitarra),* **'que'** *(vaqueros),* **'qui'** *(barquilla)*

v – pronounced like 'b': *vestido, vaca; aventura, automóvil*

z – 'th' in most of Spain: 's' in most of Latin America: *zapato, cabeza, corazón, manzana*

Pairs of letters

au –'ow': *autobús , auditorio*

ch – *chaqueta, coche*

ll – like 'li' in 'pavilion' in some regions; like 'ye' in 'yes' elsewhere: *paella, bocadillo, tortilla*

The stress marker

Words are made up of different parts, called syllables. For example, 'hamburger' has three syllables: ham-bur-ger, and the stress is on the first syllable: HAMburger.

In Spanish, a rising accent mark shows you where the stress falls to help you say it correctly: ***plástico, albóndiga, cinturón.***

Punctuation

There are two forms of Spanish punctuation that you might find strange at first, but they are easy to understand:

A question begins with an upside down question mark in Spanish: ***¿Eres español?*** – Are you Spanish?

Similarly, a phrase that might be shouted starts with an upside down exclamation mark and ends with one 'the right way up': ***¡Para ascender!*** Going up!

La familia y los amigos • *Family and friends*

Las familias pueden estar compuestas por diferente número de miembros. Hay niños que viven en familias monoparentales o con la persona que los cuida, otros tienen familias muy grandes. Los abuelos, los tíos y los primos todos ellos forman parte del clan familiar.

Families come in many sizes. Some children live with just one parent or carer. Some have large families, with many relatives. Grandparents, uncles, aunts, and cousins are all members of your extended family.

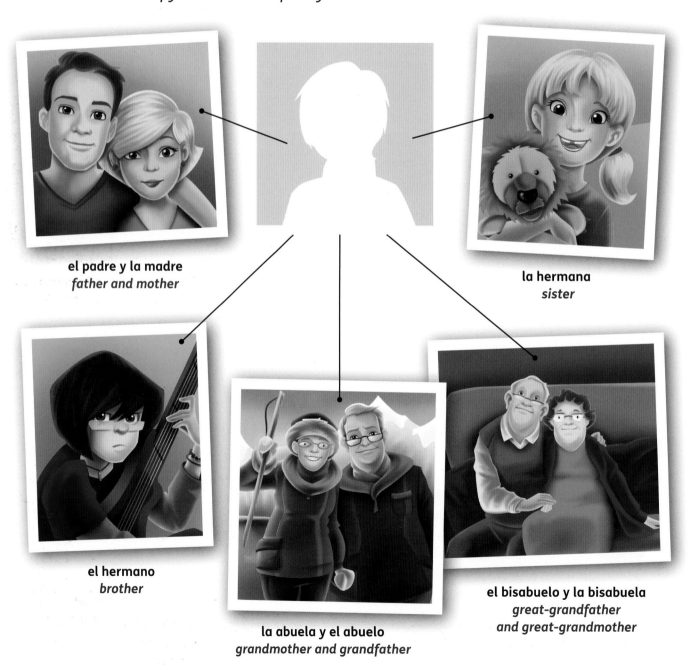

el padre y la madre
father and mother

la hermana
sister

el hermano
brother

la abuela y el abuelo
grandmother and grandfather

el bisabuelo y la bisabuela
great-grandfather and great-grandmother

People and homes

el padrastro y la madre
stepfather and mother

el tío y la tía
uncle and aunt

el(la) mejor amigo(a)
best friend

el hermanastro y la hermanastra
stepbrother and stepsister

los primos
cousins

los amigos
friends

Tu cuerpo • *Your body*

El cuerpo es una máquina increíblemente complicada. Todas las partes del cuerpo funcionan conjuntamente a la perfección para realizar diferentes tareas a la vez. ¡El cuerpo está continuamente en actividad para mantenernos vivos!

Your body is like an incredibly complicated machine. All its parts work perfectly together, so you can do many different jobs at once. It is also busy all the time keeping you alive!

La cara • *Face*

el pelo
hair

la frente
forehead

la ceja
eyebrow

el ojo
eye

la nariz
nose

la boca
mouth

la oreja
ear

las mejillas
cheeks

los dientes
teeth

la barbilla
chin

El cuerpo humano
Body

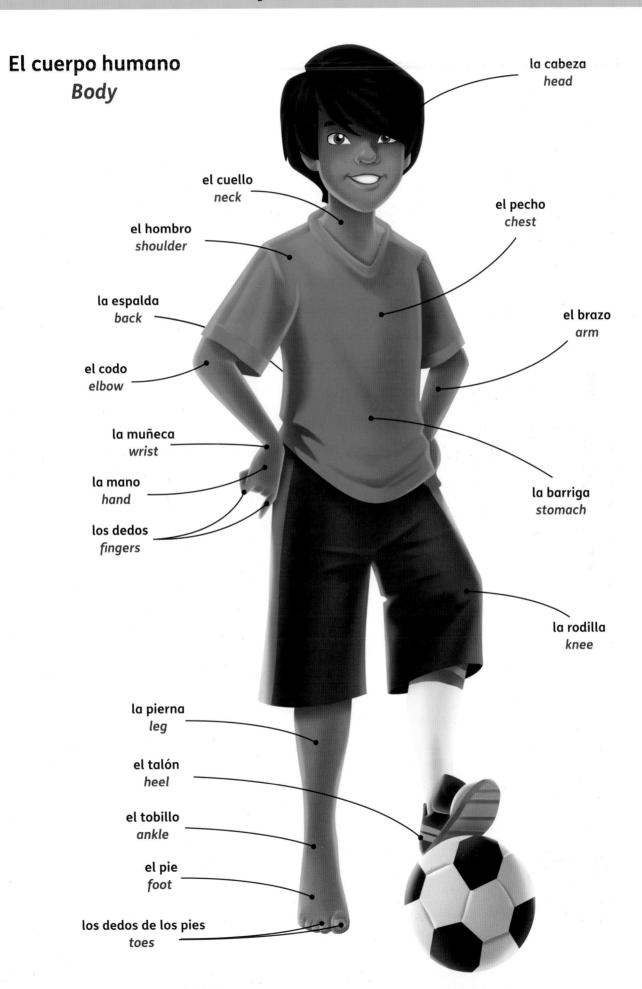

la cabeza
head

el cuello
neck

el pecho
chest

el hombro
shoulder

la espalda
back

el brazo
arm

el codo
elbow

la muñeca
wrist

la mano
hand

los dedos
fingers

la barriga
stomach

la rodilla
knee

la pierna
leg

el talón
heel

el tobillo
ankle

el pie
foot

los dedos de los pies
toes

En tu cuerpo
Inside your body

El esqueleto es el armazón que sostiene el cuerpo humano y está formado por más de 200 huesos. El esqueleto protege los órganos vitales del cuerpo (como por ejemplo el corazón y el hígado). Los músculos al tirar de los huesos hacen posible que el cuerpo se mueva.

Inside your body is your skeleton, which is made up of over 200 bones. Your skeleton protects and supports your organs (such as your heart and your liver). Your muscles pull on your bones to make your body move.

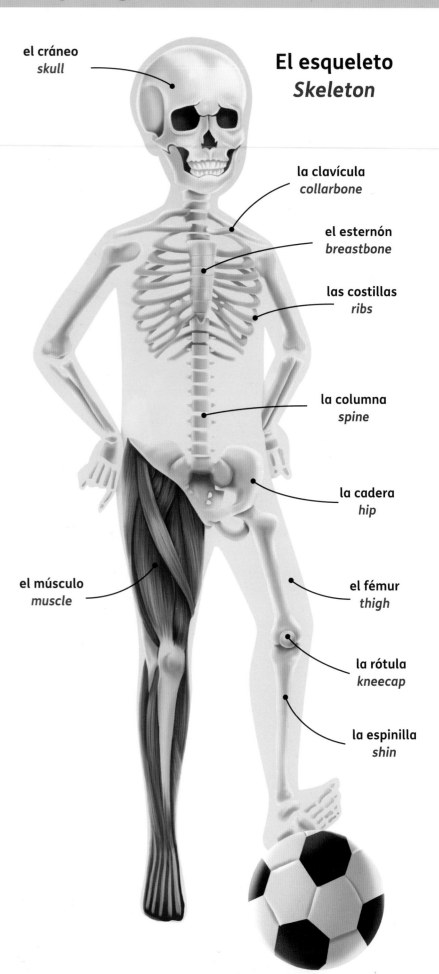

el cráneo
skull

El esqueleto
Skeleton

la clavícula
collarbone

el esternón
breastbone

las costillas
ribs

la columna
spine

la cadera
hip

el músculo
muscle

el fémur
thigh

la rótula
kneecap

la espinilla
shin

14

Los órganos

Organs

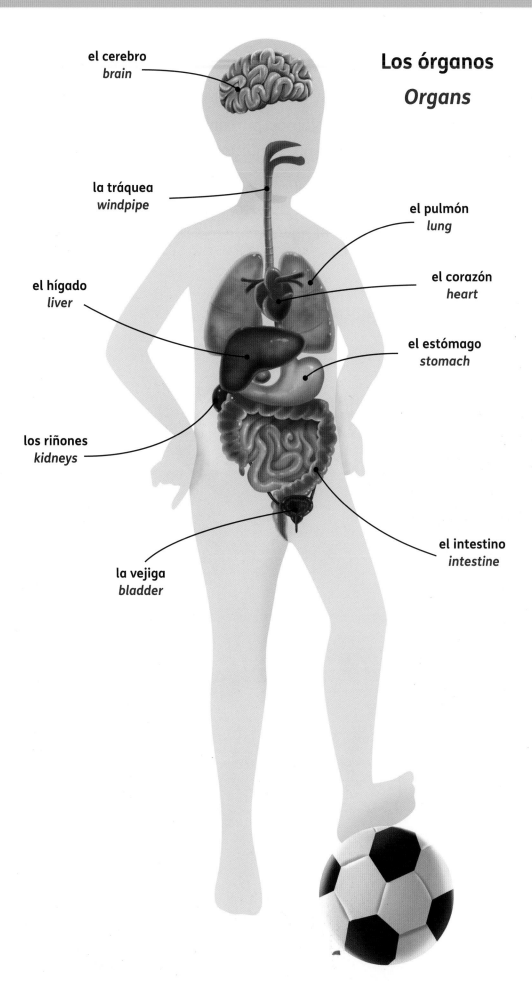

el cerebro
brain

la tráquea
windpipe

el hígado
liver

los riñones
kidneys

la vejiga
bladder

el pulmón
lung

el corazón
heart

el estómago
stomach

el intestino
intestine

Los sentidos y los sentimientos • *Senses and feelings*

Los sentidos conectan nuestro cuerpo al mundo exterior. Transmiten señales al cerebro sobre todo lo que vemos, oímos, olemos, probamos y tocamos. Usamos el rostro para transmitir señales sobre cómo nos sentimos.

Our senses link our bodies to the outside world. They carry signals to our brains about everything we see, hear, smell, taste, and touch, we use our faces to send signals to other people about how we are feeling.

El tacto • Touch

suave
soft

húmedo
wet

punzante
sharp

caliente
hot

frío
cold

El olfato • Smell

repugnante
nasty

agradable
nice

El gusto • Taste

dulce
sweet

ácido
sour

salado
salty

brillante
bright

vistoso
colourful

La vista • Sight

silencioso
quiet

fuerte
loud

El oído • Hearing

People and homes

feliz
happy

triste
sad

asustado
scared

enfadado
angry

orgulloso
proud

entusiasmado
excited

sorprendido
surprised

travieso
mischievous

tonto
silly

alegre
laughing

confuso
confused

aburrido
bored

La casa • *Home*

Hay muchos tipos de casas, algunas tienen solo una habitación mientras que otras son mansiones suntuosas; la mayoría disponen de cocina, cuarto de baño, dormitorios y salas para descansar y relajarse.

Homes come in all shapes and sizes, and range from single rooms to massive mansions. Most have areas for cooking, washing, sleeping, and relaxing.

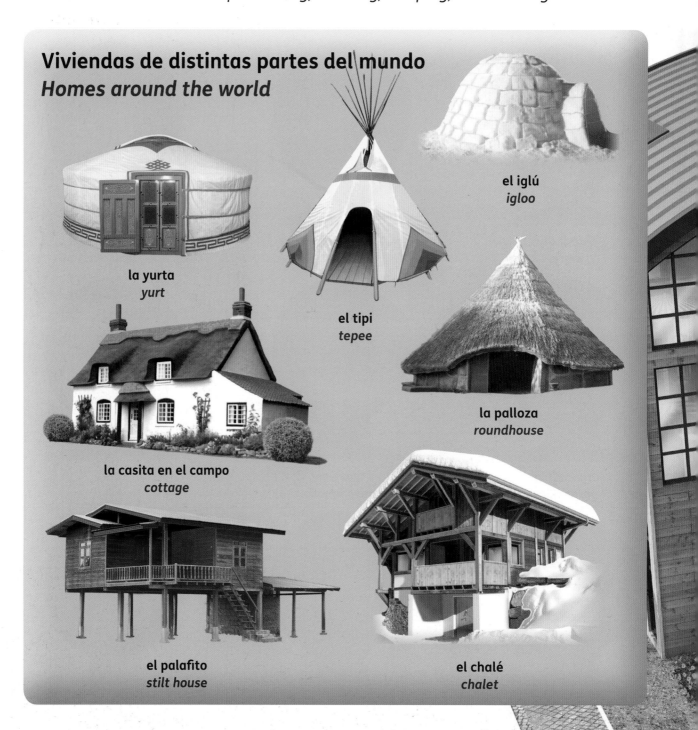

Viviendas de distintas partes del mundo
Homes around the world

el iglú
igloo

la yurta
yurt

el tipi
tepee

la palloza
roundhouse

la casita en el campo
cottage

el palafito
stilt house

el chalé
chalet

La casa

18

People and homes

1 la chimenea
chimney

2 la ventana
window

3 la puerta
door

4 el tejado
roof

5 la cocina
kitchen

6 el cuarto de baño
bathroom

7 la sala de estar
living room

8 el dormitorio
bedroom

9 el garaje
garage

10 la bañera
bath

11 el váter
toilet

12 la ducha
shower

13 la silla
chair

14 la mesa
table

15 la cama
bed

16 la televisión
television

17 el fregadero
sink

18 la cocina eléctrica/
de gas
cooker

Los artículos de la casa • *Household objects*

Nuestras casas están llenas de artículos y utensilios útiles. Estos artículos los utilizamos diariamente para cocinar y asearnos.

Our homes are full of useful household tools and materials. We use these household objects every day to cook our food and to keep ourselves clean.

En la cocina • *In the kitchen*

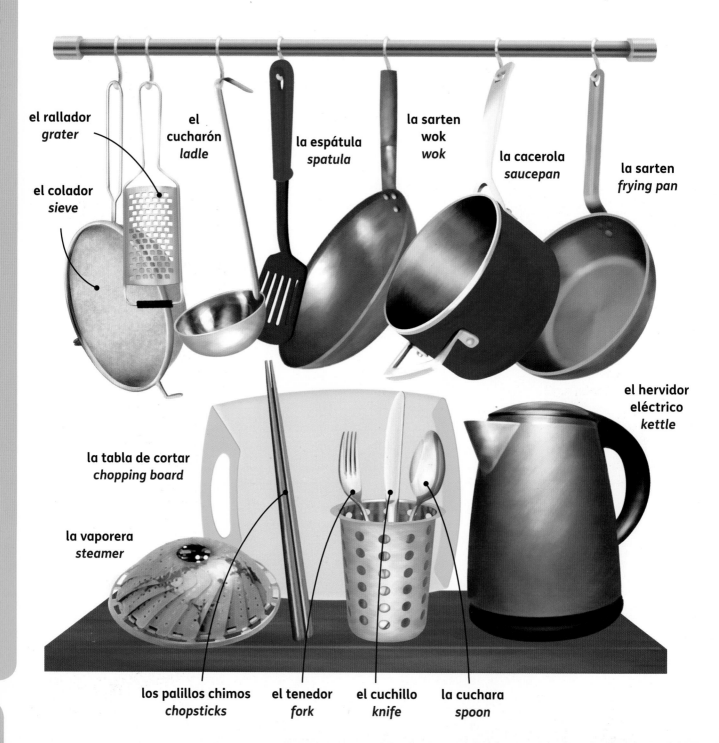

el rallador
grater

el colador
sieve

el cucharón
ladle

la espátula
spatula

la sarten wok
wok

la cacerola
saucepan

la sarten
frying pan

el hervidor eléctrico
kettle

la tabla de cortar
chopping board

la vaporera
steamer

los palillos chimos
chopsticks

el tenedor
fork

el cuchillo
knife

la cuchara
spoon

En el cuarto de baño • *In the bathroom*

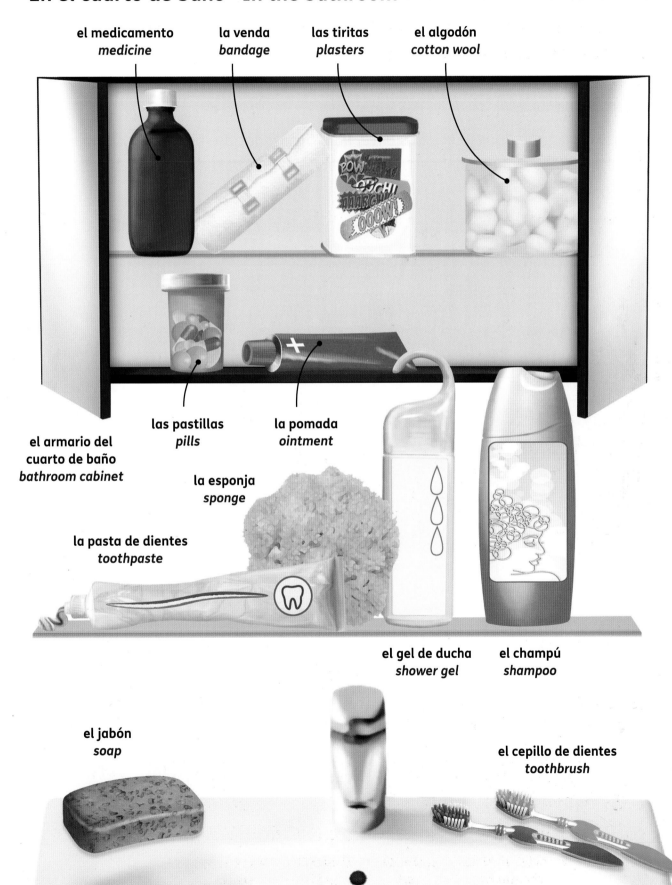

el medicamento
medicine

la venda
bandage

las tiritas
plasters

el algodón
cotton wool

las pastillas
pills

la pomada
ointment

el armario del cuarto de baño
bathroom cabinet

la esponja
sponge

la pasta de dientes
toothpaste

el gel de ducha
shower gel

el champú
shampoo

el jabón
soap

el cepillo de dientes
toothbrush

21

Comida y bebidas • *Food and drink*

Necesitamos tomar alimentos y bebidas para mantenernos vivos, pero algunos alimentos son mejores que otros para nuestra salud. La pirámide de enfrente muestra los alimentos saludables en la base y los alimentos menos saludables en la parte superior.

We need food and drink to keep us alive, but some foods are better for our health than others. The pyramid opposite shows healthy foods at the bottom and less healthy foods at the top.

Las bebidas • *Drinks*

el té verde
green tea

el chocolate a la taza
hot chocolate

el café
coffee

las bebidas con gas
fizzy drink

el zumo de fruta
fruit juice

el agua
water

el té
tea

la leche
milk

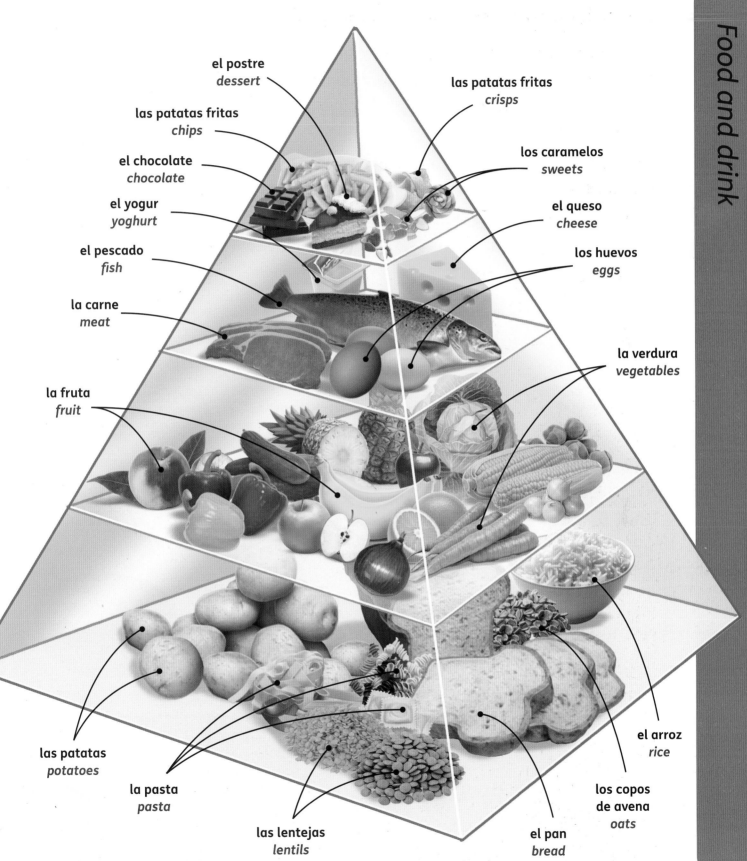

el postre
dessert

las patatas fritas
crisps

las patatas fritas
chips

los caramelos
sweets

el chocolate
chocolate

el queso
cheese

el yogur
yoghurt

el pescado
fish

los huevos
eggs

la carne
meat

la verdura
vegetables

la fruta
fruit

las patatas
potatoes

el arroz
rice

la pasta
pasta

los copos
de avena
oats

las lentejas
lentils

el pan
bread

Todo tipo de comida • *All sorts of food*

La gente toma algo ligero cuando necesitan hacer una comida rápida.
Si disponen de más tiempo, toman un plato principal y un postre.

People have a snack when they need a small meal that can be eaten fast.
If they have more time, they can enjoy a main course and a dessert.

COMIDA RÁPIDA
SNACKS

el
bocadillo
sandwich

el **wrap**
wrap

la
hamburguesa
burger

la **sopa**   el **bollo**
soup   *roll*

la **pizza**
pizza

PLATO PRINCIPAL
MAIN COURSE

el **filete**
steak

la **paella**
paella

el **cordero**
lamb

el **curry**
curry

las **albóndigas**
meatballs

el **pollo**
chicken

Platos exóticos • Weird and wonderful foods

las ancas de rana
frogs' legs

la sopa de ortigas
stinging nettle soup

las tarántulas fritas
fried tarantulas

PLATO PRINCIPAL
MAIN COURSE

la ensalada
salad

tapas
tapas

el tofu
tofu

los espaguetis
spaghetti

la tortilla
omelette

POSTRES
DESSERT

el helado
ice cream

la macedonia de frutas
fruit salad

la magdalena
cupcakes

los crepes
pancakes

la tarta
gateau

Frutas y verduras • *Fruit and vegetables*

La fruta y la verdura son las partes comestibles de las plantas. La fruta es la parte de la planta donde están las semillas, las pepitas, o el hueso. La verdura son las raíces, las hojas, o los tallos de la planta.

Fruit and vegetables are parts of plants. A fruit is the part of a plant that contains its seeds, pips, or stone. Vegetables are the roots, leaves, or stems of a plant.

las fresas
strawberries

la cebolla
onion

los pimientos
peppers

los aguacates
avocados

los guisantes
peas

los tomates
tomatoes

las zanahorias
carrots

los melocotones
peaches

los higos
figs

los limones
lemons

las calabazas
pumpkins

El interior de una manzana

Inside an apple

las pepitas *pips*

el pedúnculo *stem*

la piel *skin*

la pulpa *flesh*

las naranjas *oranges*

las cerezas *cherries*

el pepino *cucumber*

las patatas *potatoes*

los plátanos *bananas*

el maíz *sweetcorn*

el repollo *cabbage*

la sandía *watermelon*

las judías *green beans*

las peras *pears*

Ropa de diario • *Everyday clothes*

La ropa protege el cuerpo y sirve también para que estemos limpios, secos y abrigados. ¡Además, la ropa también puede ayudar a que parezcamos más guapos!

Clothes protect your body and help to keep you clean, warm, and dry. They can make you look good too!

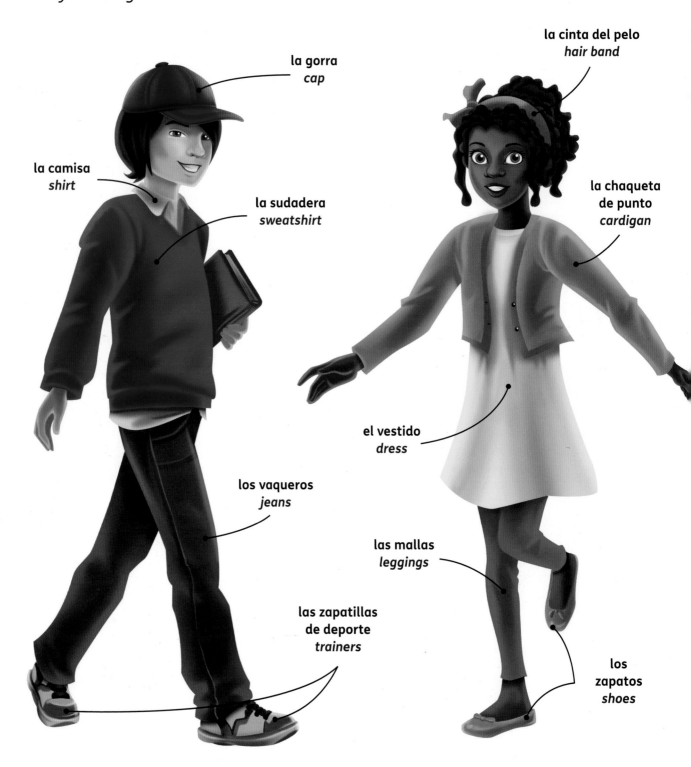

la gorra
cap

la cinta del pelo
hair band

la camisa
shirt

la chaqueta
de punto
cardigan

la sudadera
sweatshirt

el vestido
dress

los vaqueros
jeans

las mallas
leggings

las zapatillas
de deporte
trainers

los
zapatos
shoes

el gorro
hat

la bufanda
scarf

los guantes
gloves

la camiseta
T-shirt

la chaqueta de chándal
tracksuit top

el abrigo
jacket

los pantalones cortos
shorts

las medias
tights

la falda
skirt

los calcetines
socks

los botines
ankle boots

las botas de fútbol
football boots

Todo tipo de ropa • *All sorts of clothes*

En esta página vamos a ver trajes de época de la Roma antigua, de Europa y de Japón. La página siguiente muestra ropa de distintos países.

On this page you can see some historical costumes from ancient Rome, Europe, and Japan. The opposite page includes some examples of clothes from different countries.

la emperatriz japonesa
Japanese empress

el abanico
fan

el quimono
kimono

la reina medieval
medieval queen

la corona
crown

la capa
cloak

el caballero medieval
medieval knight

la coraza
breastplate

la armadura
suit of armour

el romano
ancient Roman

la toga romana
toga

las sandalias
sandals

el guerrero samurái del Japón
Japanese samurai warrior

el yelmo
helmet

el guantelete
gauntlet

la chaqueta
jacket

la falda escocesa
kilt

la blusa
blouse

el delantal
apron

el sari
sari

los zuecos
clogs

la corbata
tie

el traje
suit

el turbante
turban

el sombrero de copa
top hat

el chaleco
waistcoat

el velo de novia
veil

el vestido de novia
wedding dress

En la escuela

En la escuela • *At school*

Casi todos los niños tienen que ir a la escuela. En algunos países la edad de escolarización es a partir de los cuatro años, en otros es a partir de los siete. En la escuela se aprenden y se practican técnicas muy importantes y también se estudian varias asignaturas que ayudan a interpretar el mundo que nos rodea.

Most children have to go to school. In some countries, children start school at age four, in other countries they start at age seven. At school, you learn and practise some very important skills. You study a range of subjects that help you understand the world around you.

el reloj
clock

el horario
timetable

Merhaba
SVEIKAS BONJOUR
Xin Chao Buna Kushti Divvus
Ciao Dia Dhuit
Hej Hello TERVE
Ahoj Zdravo
Helo Jambo
Haye Kamusta
Tungjatjeta Dzien Dobry
OLYOTYA GUTEN TAG Ola
Hola

el póster
wall chart

8

4

5

6

9

3

11

12

2

10

1

7

School and work

Las clases • *Lessons*

inglés – English
historia – History
geografía – Geography
ciencias – Science
matemáticas – Maths
tecnología – Technology
música – Music
dibujo – Art

los deberes – homework
los trabajos de curso – coursework
el trabajo – project
el examen – exam

la pizarra Vileda® • *whiteboard*

1 el pupitre *desk*

2 la calculadora *calculator*

3 el cuaderno *exercise book*

4 el libro de texto *text book*

5 la carpeta de anillas *file*

6 el bloc de notas *writing pad*

7 la regla *ruler*

8 el globo *globe*

9 la grapadora *stapler*

10 el bolígrafo *pen*

11 el lápiz *pencil*

12 la goma *rubber*

Todo tipo de trabajos • *All sorts of work*

Hay muchos tipos distintos de trabajos. ¿Qué trabajo te gustaría hacer? Quizá te gustaría trabajar con ordenadores. ¿Te gustaría trabajar con animales? Imagínate la cantidad de profesiones a las que podrías dedicarte.

There are so many different types of work. What kind of work do you want to do? You may be interested in working with computers. Or would you like to work with animals? Think of all the jobs you could try.

la ingeniera
el ingeniero
engineer

la arquitecta
el arquitecto
architect

la veterinaria
el veterinario
vet

la conductora de autobús
el conductor de autobús
bus driver

School and work

**el jefe de cocina
la jefa de cocina**
chef

**el abogado
la abogada**
lawyer

**el enfermero
la enfermera**
nurse

**el reportero
la reportera**
reporter

**el agente de policía
la agente de policía**
police officer

$57 \times$
92

**el maestro
la maestra**
teacher

Equipo y ropa de trabajo • *Work equipment and clothing*

Para realizar ciertos trabajos es necesario utilizar ropa y equipo de trabajo especial. los trabajadores de la construcción, los buzos y los bomberos usan ropa especial para su seguridad personal. Los cirujanos usan ropa que impide la propagación de los microbios.

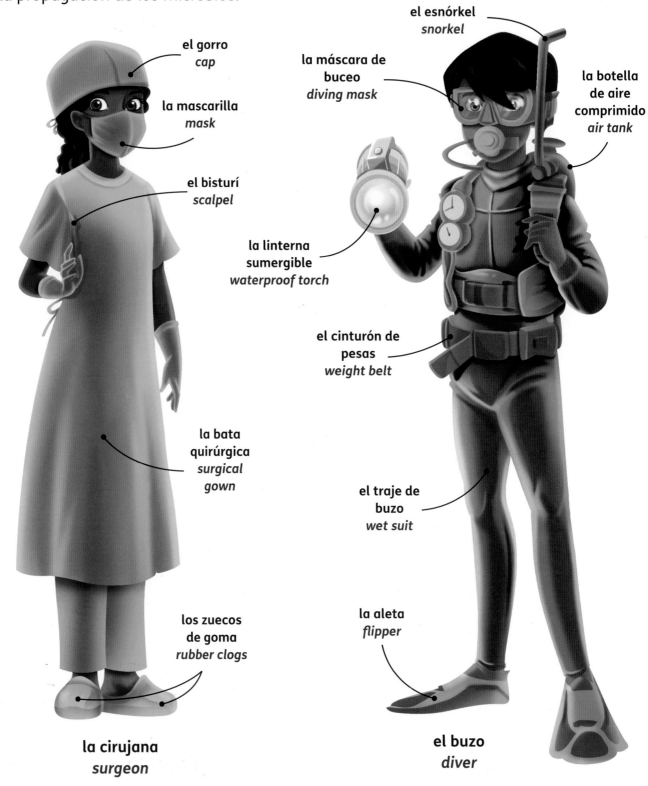

el gorro
cap

la mascarilla
mask

el bisturí
scalpel

la bata quirúrgica
surgical gown

los zuecos de goma
rubber clogs

la cirujana
surgeon

el esnórkel
snorkel

la máscara de buceo
diving mask

la botella de aire comprimido
air tank

la linterna sumergible
waterproof torch

el cinturón de pesas
weight belt

el traje de buzo
wet suit

la aleta
flipper

el buzo
diver

School and work

Some people need special equipment and clothing to do their work. Builders, divers, and firefighters wear special clothes to keep themselves safe. Surgeons wear clothing that stops germs spreading.

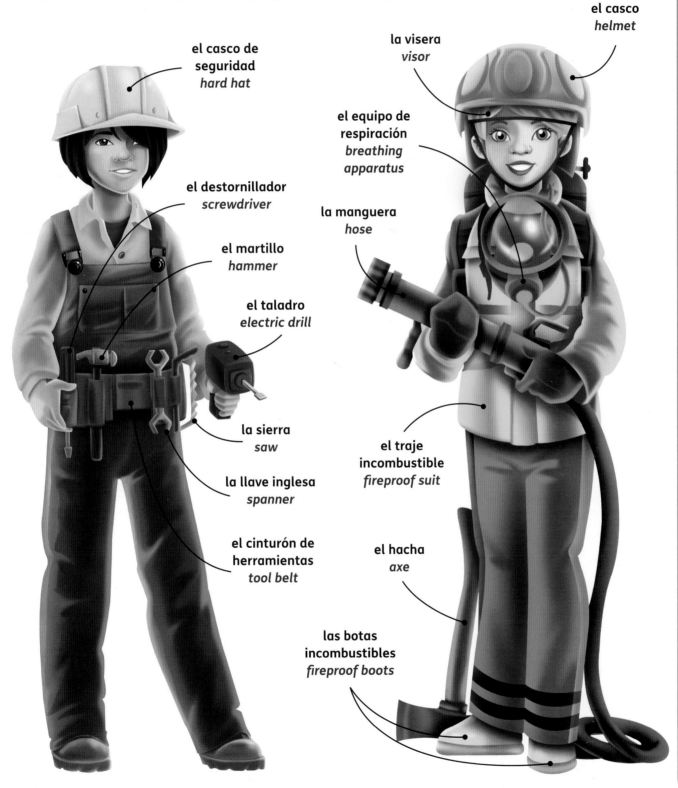

el casco de seguridad
hard hat

el destornillador
screwdriver

el martillo
hammer

el taladro
electric drill

la sierra
saw

la llave inglesa
spanner

el cinturón de herramientas
tool belt

el albañil
builder

la visera
visor

el casco
helmet

el equipo de respiración
breathing apparatus

la manguera
hose

el traje incombustible
fireproof suit

el hacha
axe

las botas incombustibles
fireproof boots

la bombera
firefighter

Deporte • *Sports*

El deporte es muy importante, nos ayuda a mantenernos en forma y es divertido practicarlo. Los atletas profesionales de todo el mundo entrenan mucho para participar en las principales competiciones, como las Olimpiadas. Hay dos Olimpiadas – una en verano y otra en invierno.

Sport is important, it keeps us fit and is fun. Professional athletes all over the world train hard to compete in top competitions, such as the Olympics. There are two Olympics – one in summer and one in winter.

el fútbol
football

el tenis
tennis

el béisbol
baseball

el rugby
rugby

la gimnasia
gymnastics

el voleibol
volleyball

el tiro con arco
archery

el ciclismo
cycling

el atletismo
athletics

El fútbol • Football

el árbitro • *referee*

parar • *to save*

marcar • *to score*

el gol • *goal*

el penalti • *penalty*

el tiro libre • *free kick*

el, la defensa • *defender*

el portero, la portera • *goalkeeper*

el delantero, la delantera • *striker*

el baloncesto
basketball

el yudo
judo

el críquet
cricket

el golf
golf

la natación
swimming

el hockey sobre hielo
ice hockey

Deporte en acción • *Sports in action*

La participación en cualquier deporte exige mucha actividad. Correr es la base de muchos deportes, pero también hay otras muchas actividades y ejercicios.

Taking part in any kind of sport means a lot of action! Running is part of many sports but there are many other activities too.

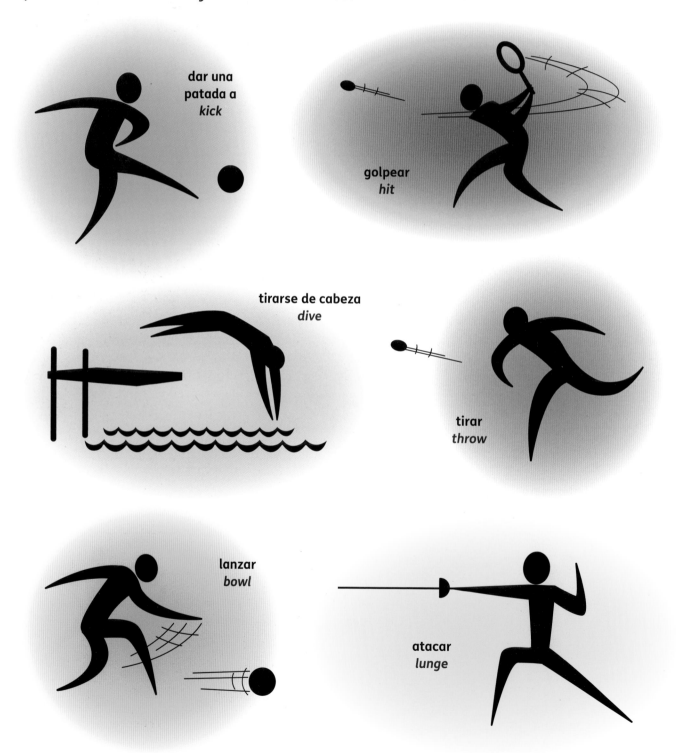

dar una patada a
kick

golpear
hit

tirarse de cabeza
dive

tirar
throw

lanzar
bowl

atacar
lunge

coger
catch

disparar
shoot

saltar
jump

deslizarse
glide

patinar
skate

**montar
(a caballo)**
ride

remar
paddle

Juegos y pasatiempos
Games and leisure

A lo largo de la historia el hombre ha practicado diferentes tipos de juegos. Son juegos muy antiguos el ajedrez, las cometas y el yoyó. Los juegos electrónicos son mucho más recientes.

People all over the world have been playing games for centuries. Chess, kites, and yo-yos have a very long history. Electronic games are a recent invention.

1 el monopatín
skateboard

2 los patines en línea
rollerblades

3 el balón
football

4 la raqueta
racket

5 el volante
shuttlecock

6 el bate
bat

7 el yoyó
yo-yo

8 la cometa
kite

9 las bolas de malabares
juggling balls

10 el tablero de ajedrez
chessboard

11 la pieza de ajedrez
chess pieces

12 los auriculares
earphones

13 el puzzle
jigsaw puzzle

14 el juego de mesa
board game

15 la revista
magazine

16 la novela
novel

17 el DVD
DVD

18 el reproductor de música
music player

19 la videoconsola
games console

20 la maqueta
model

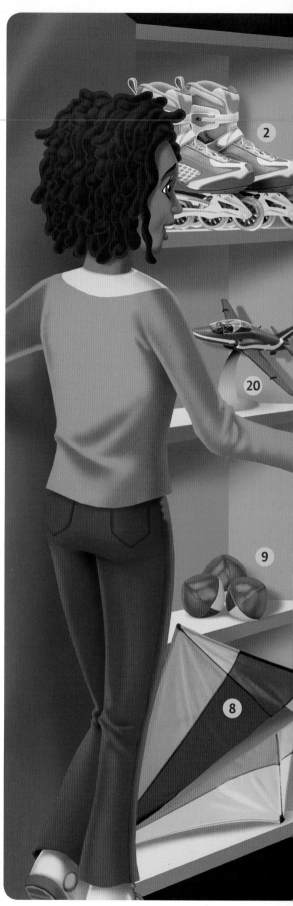

Artes plásticas, música y espectáculos

Artes plásticas y manualidades • *Art*

La gente crea arte observando lo que les rodea, o utilizando la imaginación. Se pueden utilizar diferentes recursos, como pinturas, cámaras, arcilla o incluso mármol, para crear obras de arte. La obra de artistas famosos se puede contemplar en los diferentes museos del mundo.

People create art by observing what they see around them, or by using their imagination. We can use paints, cameras, clay, or even marble to create art. You can see the work of famous artists in galleries around the world.

el retrato
portrait

el esbozo
sketch

la fotografía
photograph

el bodegón
still life

el paisaje
landscape

los dibujos animados
cartoon

Art, music, and entertainment

Herramientas del artista • *Artist's equipment*

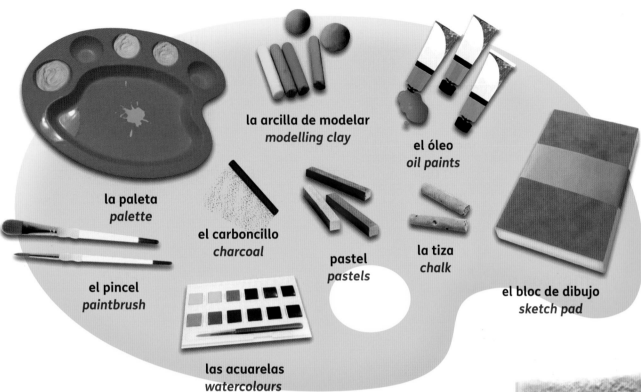

la arcilla de modelar
modelling clay

el óleo
oil paints

la paleta
palette

el carboncillo
charcoal

pastel
pastels

la tiza
chalk

el pincel
paintbrush

el bloc de dibujo
sketch pad

las acuarelas
watercolours

el vidrio de colores
stained glass

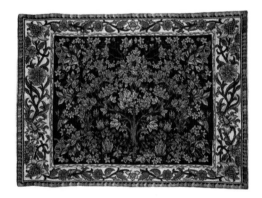

el tapiz
tapestry

el grafiti
graffiti

la escultura
sculpture

Artes plásticas, música y espectáculos

Instrumentos musicales • *Musical instruments*

Hay cuatro tipos principales de instrumentos musicales. Los instrumentos de cuerda tienen cuerdas que suenan punteándolas o haciendo que un arco las roce; los instrumentos provistos de teclado suenan pulsando las teclas; los de viento suenan impulsando aire dentro de ellos y a los de percusión se les hace sonar golpeándolos.

There are four main types of musical instruments. Stringed instruments have strings to pluck or play with a bow. Keyboard instruments have keys to press. Wind instruments are played by blowing air through them. Percussion instruments are banged to make noise.

Instrumentos de viento
Wind instruments

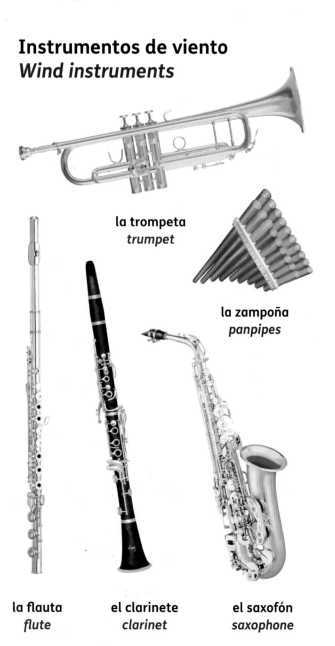

la trompeta
trumpet

la zampoña
panpipes

la flauta
flute

el clarinete
clarinet

el saxofón
saxophone

Instrumentos de teclado
Keyboard instruments

el sintetizador
synthesizer

el órgano
organ

el piano
piano

Art, music, and entertainment

Instrumentos de cuerda • *Stringed instruments*

el sitar
sitar

el arco
bow

el contrabajo
double-bass

el chelo
cello

el violín
violin

el arpa
harp

la guitarra
guitar

Instrumentos de percusión
Percussion instruments

las maracas
maracas

la pandereta
tambourine

los platillos
cymbals

la batería
drums

la tabla
tabla

Música y baile • *Music and dance*

En todo el mundo la gente compone y crea distintos tipos de música y de bailes. La música puede ser interpretada por una orquesta grande, por un grupo pequeño o por un solo músico y también podemos bailar solos, en pareja o en grupo.

People around the world love to create different types of music and dance. Music can be played by a large orchestra, by a small band, or by a solo performer. You can dance alone, with a partner, or in a group.

la música clásica
classical music

el rock
rock

el jazz
jazz

el pop
pop

la música folk
folk

Art, music, and entertainment

el reggae
reggae

el rap
rap

el soul
soul

la música global
world music

Baile • *Dance*

el claqué
tap dancing

el breakdance
breakdancing

el baile de salón
ballroom dancing

el ballet
ballet

Televisión, cine y teatro
TV, film, and theatre

Trabajar en equipo es fundamental para hacer programas de televisión, películas o teatro. Se necesita mucha gente y aparatos para filmar un espectáculo en directo, como por ejemplo un programa concurso en un auditorio.

Teamwork is important when a show is being made for television, cinema, or the theatre. A lot of people and equipment are needed to film a live event, such as a talent show in a theatre.

1 el cámara
camera operator

2 el técnico de sonido
sound engineer

3 el director
director

4 la cámara
camera

5 el escenario
stage

6 el foco
spotlight

7 el micrófono
microphone

8 el, la cantante
singer

9 el bailarín, la bailarina
dancer

10 el actor, la actriz
actor

11 el vestuario
costume

12 el decorado
scenery

13 el director de escena, la directora de escena
stage manager

14 el monitor
monitor screen

15 la claqueta
clapperboard

16 el telón
curtains

17 el productor, la productora
producer

18 el público
audience

Programas de televisión y películas • *TV shows and films*

¿Qué tipo de películas y de programas de televisión te gustan? ¿Cuáles te gustan más: las películas de humor o las películas que te hacen reflexionar? Algunas películas y programas de televisión muestran acontecimientos reales. Otros muestran situaciones imaginarias.

What kind of films and TV shows do you like? Do you prefer comedies or films that make you think? Some films and TV programmes show real events. Others show imaginary situations.

una película de terror
horror

una película de ciencia ficción y fantasía
science fiction and fantasy

una película de acción y de aventuras
action and adventure

una comedia
comedy

Art, music, and entertainment

los dibujos animados
cartoon

las noticias
news programme

un programa deportivo
sports programme

una tertulia
talk show

un documental de la naturaleza
nature documentary

un programa concurso
game show

Vehículos de pasajeros

Vehículos de pasajeros • *Passenger vehicles*

Hay muchas formas diferentes de viajar. Puedes viajar utilizando el transporte público, como por ejemplo el tren, el autobús, o el metro, o utilizando tu vehículo particular, como la bicicleta o el coche.

There are many ways to travel. You can go by public transport, such as the train, bus, or tube, or you can use your own vehicle, such as a bicycle or a car.

Las partes de un coche • *Parts of a car*

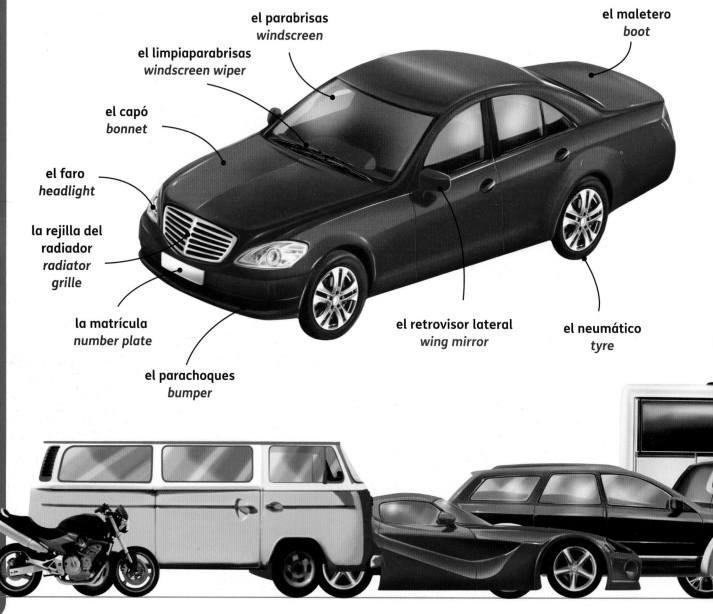

el parabrisas
windscreen

el maletero
boot

el limpiaparabrisas
windscreen wiper

el capó
bonnet

el faro
headlight

la rejilla del radiador
radiator grille

la matrícula
number plate

el parachoques
bumper

el retrovisor lateral
wing mirror

el neumático
tyre

la moto
motorbike

la autocaravana
campervan

el coche deportivo
sports car

el coche familiar
estate car

¡Hacia arriba! • *Going up!*

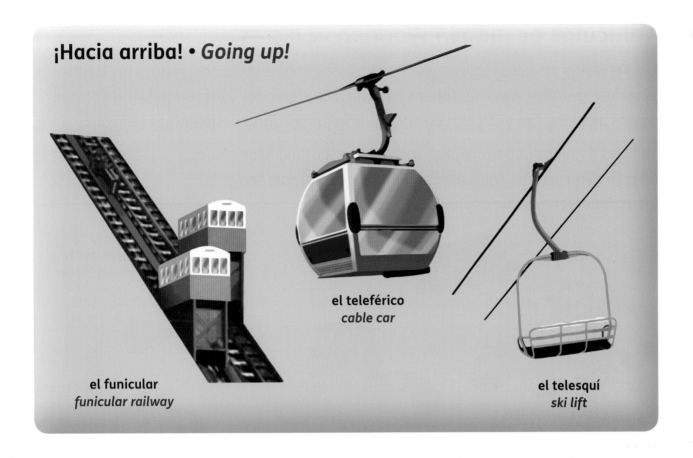

el funicular
funicular railway

el teleférico
cable car

el telesquí
ski lift

el tren • *train*

el autocar
coach

el SUV
SUV

la motocicleta
moped

el taxi
taxi

la bicicleta
bicycle

Vehículos pesados • *Working vehicles*

Los vehículos pesados realizan muchos trabajos importantes, tales como transportar cargas pesadas, levantar pesos, apisonar y excavar. Los camiones y los tanques transportan cargas pesadas. Los vehículos de emergencia proporcionan asistencia esencial.

Vehicles do many important jobs, such as transporting heavy loads, lifting, rolling and digging. Lorries and tankers transport heavy loads. Emergency vehicles provide essential help.

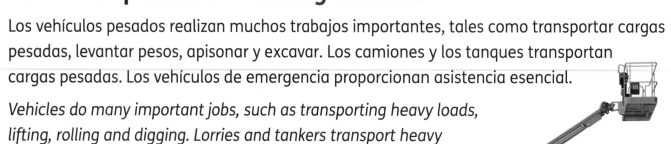

la grúa con cesta
cherry picker

la pala retroexcavadora
backhoe loader

la apisonadora
roller

la carretilla elevadora
forklift truck

la excavadora
excavator

la motoniveladora
bulldozer

el camión volquete
dumper truck

la grúa mecánica
crane

Travel and transport

la ambulancia
ambulance

el coche de bomberos
fire engine

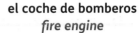

el vehículo anfibio
amphibious vehicle

la motonieve
snowmobile

**la furgoneta
de reparto**
delivery van

el coche patrulla
police car

**el camión
portacontenedores**
skip truck

el camión portacoches
car transporter

el quitanieves
snow plough

el camión hormigonera
mixer truck

el vehículo pesado
heavy goods vehicle

Aeronaves • *Aircraft*

Las aeronaves están propulsadas por motores a reacción, por hélices, o por palas de rotor. Los globos aerostáticos ascienden porque están llenos de aire de menos densidad que el aire que les rodea. Los planeadores se desplazan aprovechando las corrientes térmicas ascendientes de aire caliente para volar.

Aircraft are powered by jet engines, by propellers, or by rotor blades. A hot air balloon rises up because the air inside its envelope is lighter than the surrounding air. Gliders ride on currents of air, called thermals.

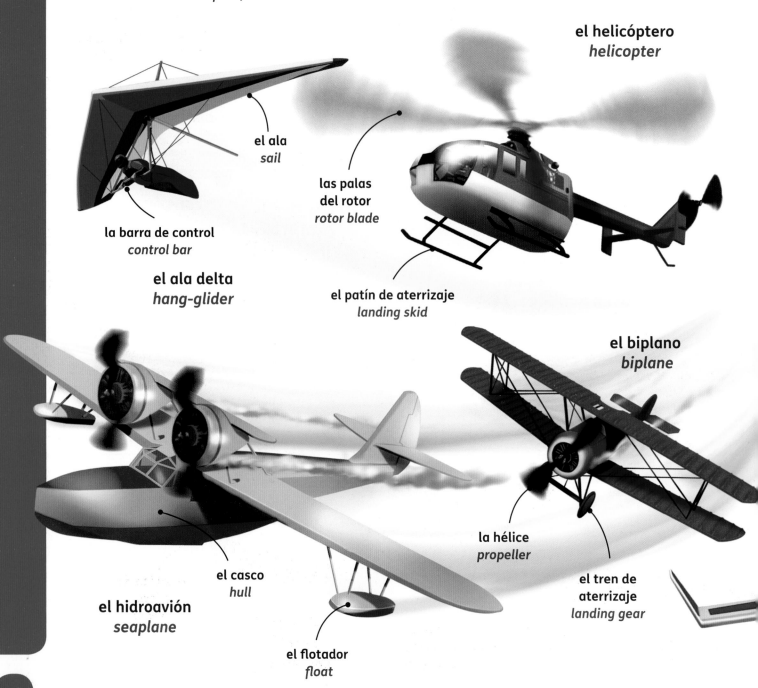

el helicóptero
helicopter

el ala
sail

las palas del rotor
rotor blade

la barra de control
control bar

el ala delta
hang-glider

el patín de aterrizaje
landing skid

el biplano
biplane

la hélice
propeller

el casco
hull

el hidroavión
seaplane

el tren de aterrizaje
landing gear

el flotador
float

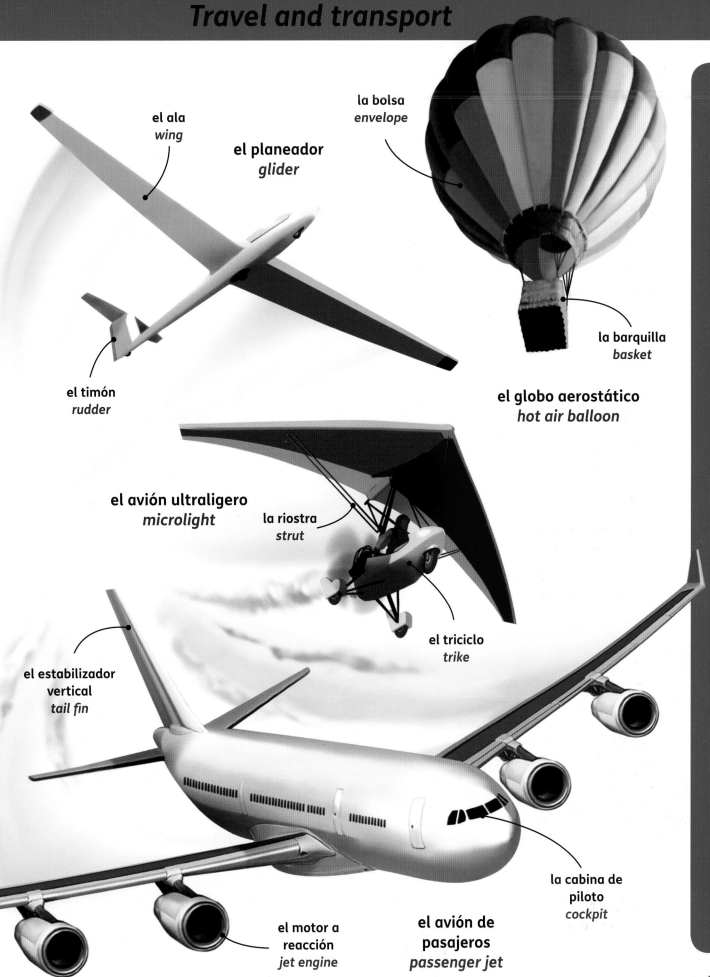

el ala
wing

el planeador
glider

la bolsa
envelope

el timón
rudder

la barquilla
basket

el globo aerostático
hot air balloon

el avión ultraligero
microlight

la riostra
strut

el triciclo
trike

el estabilizador
vertical
tail fin

la cabina de
piloto
cockpit

el motor a
reacción
jet engine

**el avión de
pasajeros**
passenger jet

Buques, barcos y otras embarcaciones
Ships, boats, and other craft

Hoy día, casi todas las embarcaciones y los barcos grandes cuentan con algún tipo de motor. Los veleros utilizan el viento para desplazarse. Los botes de remos tienen varios remos y las canoas palas.

Today, most large ships and boats have some kind of engine. Sailing boats rely on wind power. A rowing boat has a set of oars, and a canoe has a paddle.

el hidrodeslizador
hydrofoil

el buque cisterna
tanker

la vela
sail

el mástil
mast

el ferry
ferry

la lancha motora
motor boat

la botavara
boom

la tabla de windsurf
sailboard

el yate
yacht

Las partes de un barco
Parts of a ship

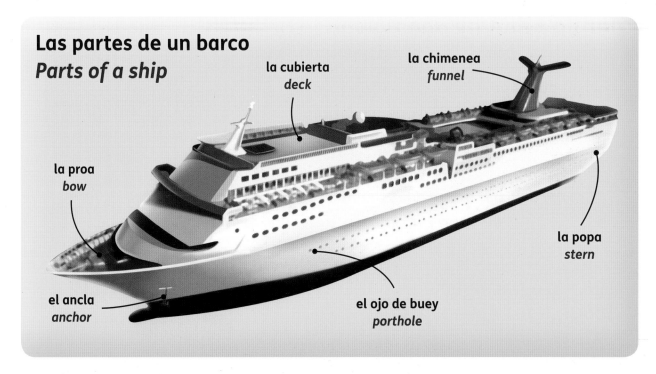

la cubierta
deck

la chimenea
funnel

la proa
bow

la popa
stern

el ancla
anchor

el ojo de buey
porthole

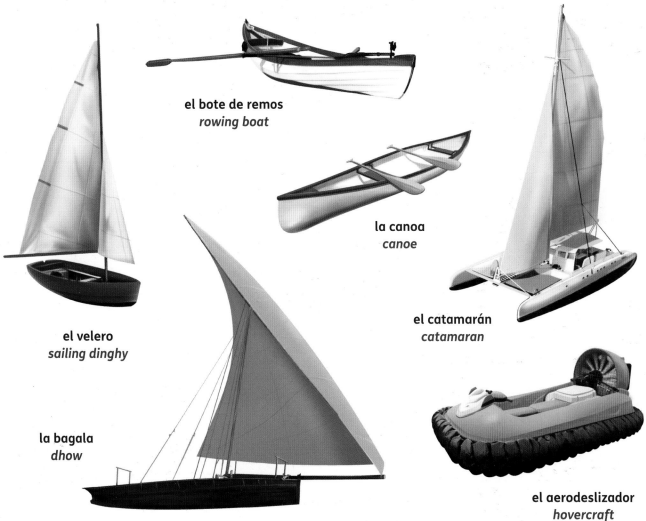

el bote de remos
rowing boat

la canoa
canoe

el velero
sailing dinghy

el catamarán
catamaran

la bagala
dhow

el aerodeslizador
hovercraft

Energía • *Energy and power*

Dependemos de la energía para abastecer de luz y calefacción a nuestros hogares y también para hacer funcionar los aparatos que usamos diariamente; pero ¿de dónde procede la energía? La energía procede de varias fuentes; se transforma en electricidad y se suministra a nuestros hogares.

We rely on energy to supply our homes with light and heat and to run the machines we use every day. But where does that energy come from? Energy comes from a range of sources. It is converted into electricity and delivered to our homes.

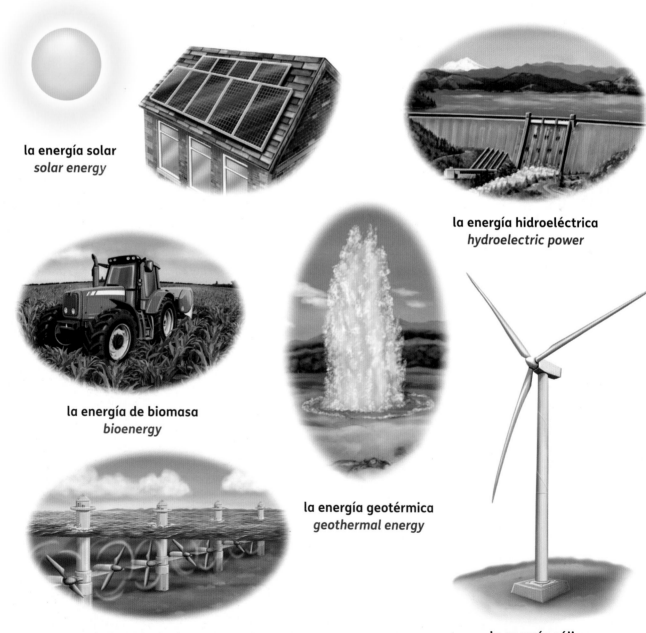

la energía solar
solar energy

la energía hidroeléctrica
hydroelectric power

la energía de biomasa
bioenergy

la energía geotérmica
geothermal energy

la energía de las mareas
tidal energy

la energía eólica
wind power

el petróleo
oil

el carbón
coal

el gas natural
natural gas

la energía nuclear
nuclear energy

Símbolos de un circuito eléctrico • *Electrical circuit symbols*

La corriente eléctrica pasa por un circuito. El circuito incluye varios componentes, como por ejemplo un interruptor, un hilo conductor y una lámpara. Los circuitos se pueden representar en forma de diagramas. Los diagramas de los circuitos tienen símbolos para representar cada componente.

Electricity runs through a circuit. The circuit includes several components or parts, such as a switch, a wire, and a light bulb. Electrical circuits can be shown as diagrams. Circuit diagrams have symbols to represent each component.

diagrama de un circuito eléctrico • *circuit diagram*

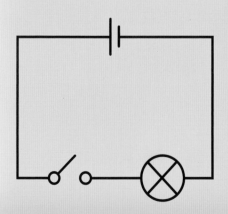

la pila
battery

el hilo conductor
wire

la lámpara
bulb

el timbre
buzzer

el motor
motor

el interruptor (abierto)
switch (off)

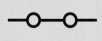

el interruptor (cerrado)
switch (on)

Todo tipo de materiales • *All kinds of materials*

Los materiales tienen propiedades muy diferentes; los hay pesados o ligeros, flexibles o rígidos. Algunos tienen propiedades magnéticas (atraen objetos hechos de hierro); otros son buenos conductores de la electricidad y los hay con propiedades aislantes que se usan para aislamiento eléctrico.

Materials have different properties. They may be heavy or light, flexible or rigid. A few materials are magnetic (able to attract objects made of iron). Some materials are good conductors and allow an electric current to pass through them. Others are insulators and block electric currents.

| el cristal
glass | la piel
leather | el papel
paper | el plástico
plastic | el caucho
rubber |

| la porcelana
china | la madera
wood | la cera
wax | la lana
wool | el algodón
cotton |

Science and technology

Propiedades de los materiales
Properties of materials

duro • hard
blando • soft
transparente • transparent
opaco • opaque
áspero • rough
brillante • shiny
liso • smooth

magnético • magnetic
apagado • dull
impermeable • waterproof
absorbente • absorbent

el oro
gold

la plata
silver

el bronce
bronze

la piedra
stone

el latón
brass

el hierro
iron

el acero
steel

el cobre
copper

Edificios y estructuras • *Buildings and structures*

Los edificios y las estructuras tienen que ser muy fuertes. Se construyen con una amplia gama de materiales. Los constructores usan piedra, madera, ladrillos, hormigón, acero, cristal o una combinación de estos materiales.

Buildings and structures need to be very strong. They can be constructed from a wide range of materials. Builders may use stone, wood, bricks, concrete, steel, or glass, or a combination of these materials.

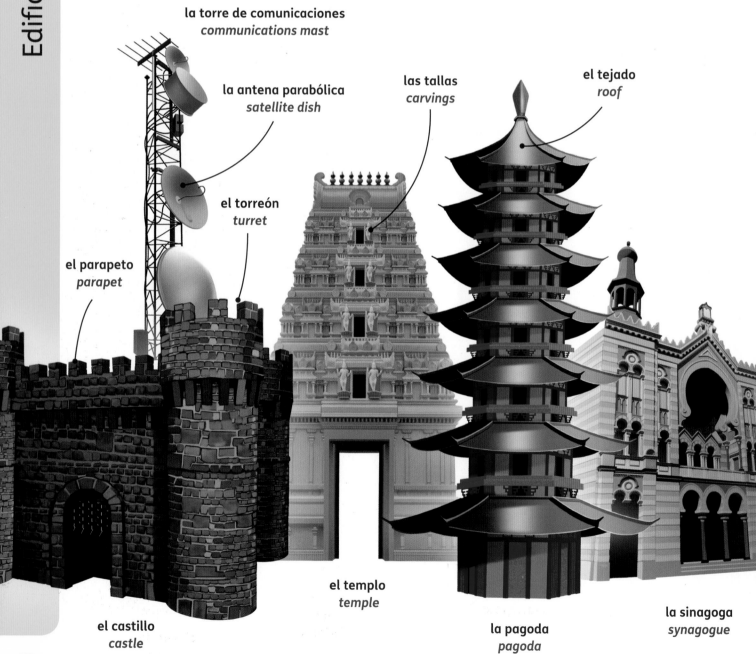

la torre de comunicaciones
communications mast

la antena parabólica
satellite dish

las tallas
carvings

el tejado
roof

el torreón
turret

el parapeto
parapet

el templo
temple

el castillo
castle

la pagoda
pagoda

la sinagoga
synagogue

Science and technology

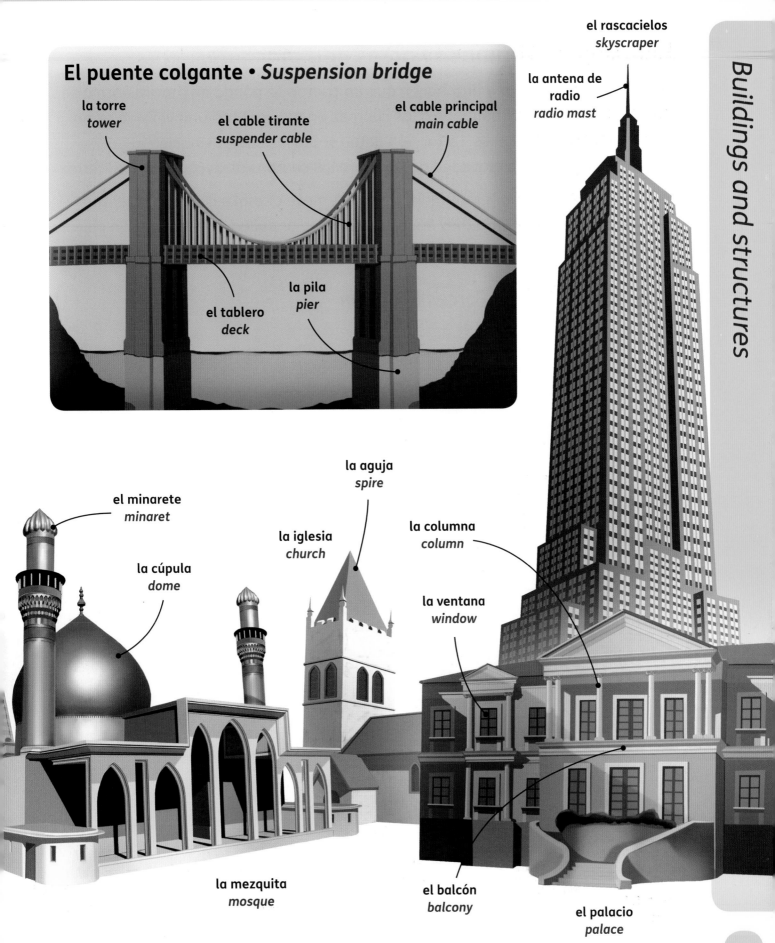

El puente colgante • *Suspension bridge*

la torre
tower

el cable tirante
suspender cable

el cable principal
main cable

el tablero
deck

la pila
pier

el rascacielos
skyscraper

la antena de radio
radio mast

el minarete
minaret

la cúpula
dome

la iglesia
church

la aguja
spire

la columna
column

la ventana
window

la mezquita
mosque

el balcón
balcony

el palacio
palace

Fuerzas y máquinas • *Forces and machines*

Las fuerzas de empujar y tirar hacen que un cuerpo se ponga en movimiento o se detenga. El momento mantiene a los cuerpos en movimiento una vez que se ha empujado o tirado de ellos. La fricción actúa sobre los cuerpos haciendo que se paren y la fuerza de la gravedad actúa sobre los cuerpos atrayéndolos a la Tierra.

Forces are pushes or pulls that make an object move or make it stop. Momentum keeps objects moving after they have been pushed or pulled. Friction acts on objects to make them stop moving. The force of gravity pulls objects down towards the Earth.

Fuerzas en acción • *Forces in action*

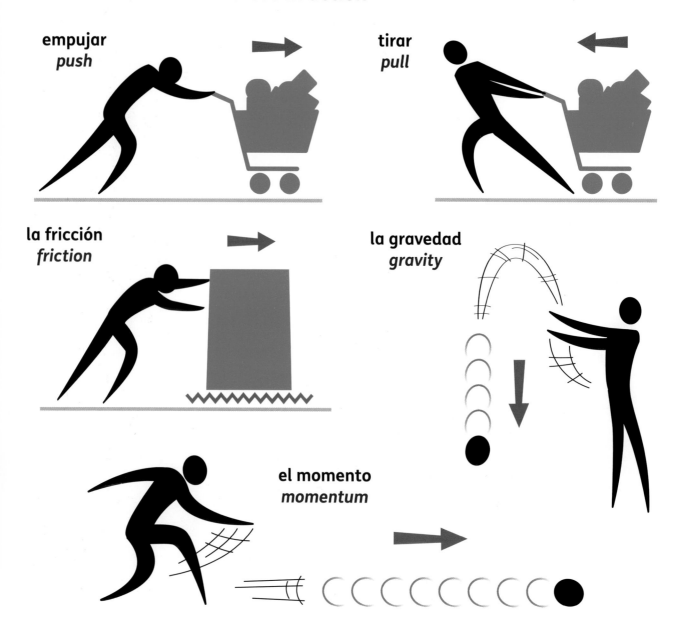

empujar
push

tirar
pull

la fricción
friction

la gravedad
gravity

el momento
momentum

Máquinas sencillas • *Simple machines*

Empujando y tirando se pueden levantar pesos pesados con máquinas sencillas.

Pushes and pulls can be used in machines to lift heavy loads.

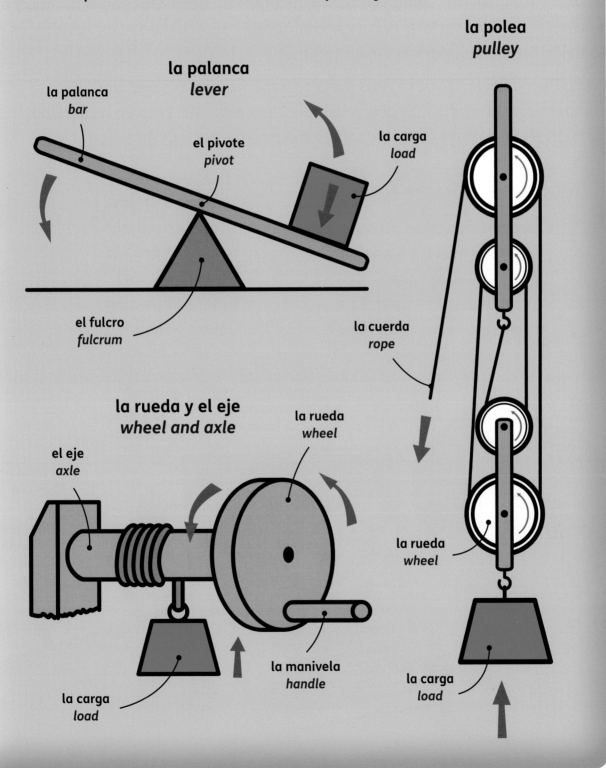

la palanca
bar

la palanca
lever

el pivote
pivot

la carga
load

el fulcro
fulcrum

la polea
pulley

la cuerda
rope

la rueda y el eje
wheel and axle

el eje
axle

la rueda
wheel

la rueda
wheel

la manivela
handle

la carga
load

la carga
load

Ordenadores y dispositivos electrónicos
Computers and electronic devices

Los ordenadores y los dispositivos electrónicos han transformado nuestro modo de vivir y trabajar. Nos comunicamos al instante con gente de todo el mundo y a través de las redes sociales nos mantenemos en contacto con nuestros amigos, y también buscamos información en Internet.

Computers and electronic devices transform the way we live and work. We communicate instantly with people all over the world. We keep up with friends through social networks, and we search the Internet for information.

En Internet • *On the Internet*

el archivo adjunto • *attachment*
la página inicial • *home page*
el chat • *chat*
conectar • *connect*
el correo electrónico • *email*
el blog • *blog*

twitear • *tweet*
buscar • *search*
explorar • *browse*
navegar • *surf*
bajar • *download*
subir • *upload*
wifi • *wi-fi*

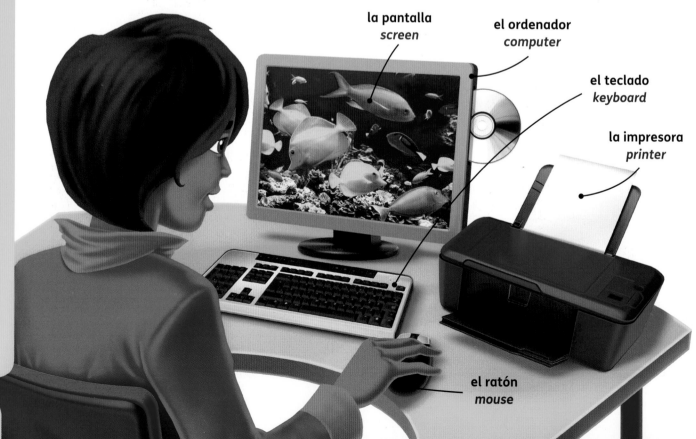

la pantalla
screen

el ordenador
computer

el teclado
keyboard

la impresora
printer

el ratón
mouse

**el reproductor
de MP3**
MP3 player

**el teléfono
móvil**
mobile phone

la llave USB
memory stick

la cámara digital
digital camera

el tablet
tablet

**el ordenador
portátil**
laptop

el ereader
e-reader

Operaciones en el ordenador • *Computer actions*

conectar • *connect*	**insertar** • *insert*
iniciar sesión • *log on*	**borrar** • *delete*
cerrar sesión • *log off*	**formatear** • *format*
teclear • *type*	**editar** • *edit*
desplazarse • *scroll*	**pasar el corrector ortográfico** • *spell check*
hacer clic • *click*	**imprimir** • *print*
arrastrar • *drag*	**escanear** • *scan*
cortar • *cut*	**guardar** • *save*
pegar • *paste*	**hacer una copia de seguridad** • *back up*

Mamíferos • *Mammals*

Los mamíferos se caracterizan por tener sangre caliente, es decir tienen temperatura constante incluso cuando el ambiente sea frío. Las crías se desarrollan en el interior de las hembras (en lugar de en un huevo) y son amamantadas por la madre. Hay mamíferos de todos los tamaños, desde ratones y murciélagos diminutos hasta elefantes, ballenas y delfines enormes.

Mammals are warm-blooded, which means they can stay warm even in cold surroundings. Female mammals give birth to live babies (rather than eggs) and feed their babies with milk. Mammals range in size from tiny mice and bats to enormous elephants, whales, and dolphins.

el mono
monkey

la girafa
giraffe

el elefante
elephant

el camello
camel

el rinoceronte
rhinoceros

el oso polar
polar bear

el hipopótamo
hippopotamus

el leopardo
leopard

Raros y extraordinarios
Unusual and extraordinary

el topo de nariz estrellada
star-nosed mole

el ornitorrinco
duck-billed platypus

el pangolín
pangolin

el perezoso
sloth

la cebra
zebra

la llama
llama

el ciervo
deer

la ardilla
squirrel

la ardilla listada
chipmunk

el gorila
gorilla

el león
lion

la pantera
panther

el canguro
kangaroo

el guepardo
cheetah

Animales domésticos • *Working animals*

Algunos animales viven en contacto directo con el hombre. Los animales grandes de labor tiran o acarrean cargas pesadas. Los perros realizan tareas útiles, como arrear las ovejas, rastrear, o cazar. Los animales domésticos nos proporcionan carne, leche o huevos y mucha gente los tienen como mascotas.

Some animals live very closely with people. Large working animals pull or carry heavy loads. Dogs perform many useful tasks, such as herding sheep, tracking, or hunting. Farm animals are kept for their meat or for their milk or eggs, and many people like to keep animals as pets.

el búfalo de agua
water buffalo

el caballo
horse

la cabra
goat

el perro pastor
sheepdog

la oveja
sheep

Animals and plants

Animales pequeños
Small animals

el ratón
mouse

el hámster
hamster

el loro
parrot

el conejillo de Indias
guinea pig

el periquito
budgerigar

la vaca
cow

el burro
donkey

el pato
duck

el pavo
turkey

el ganso
goose

el perro de rescate de montaña
mountain-rescue dog

el gato
cat

la gallina
hen

el gallo
cockerel

Reptiles y anfibios • *Reptiles and amphibians*

Los reptiles ponen huevos y tienen el cuerpo cubierto de escamas. Son reptiles los cocodrilos, las tortugas y las serpientes. Los anfibios tienen la piel suave y normalmente parece que está mojada. Se reproducen en el agua, pero viven fuera. Son anfibios los sapos, las ranas y los tritones.

Reptiles lay eggs and have scaly skin. They include crocodiles, tortoises, and snakes. Amphibians have smooth skin that usually feels damp. They live on land but breed in water. Amphibians include toads, frogs, and newts.

la tortuga marina
turtle

la tortuga
tortoise

el lagarto
lizard

la iguana
iguana

el camaleón
chameleon

el dragón de Komodo
Komodo dragon

la salamandra
salamander

Serpientes • *Snakes*

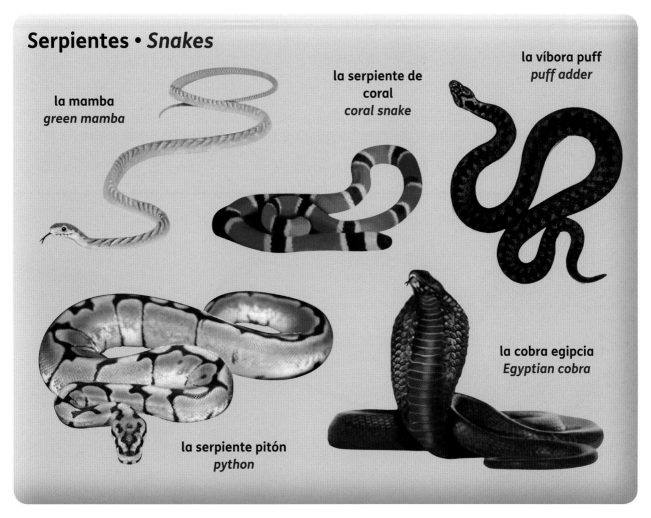

la mamba
green mamba

la serpiente de coral
coral snake

la víbora puff
puff adder

la serpiente pitón
python

la cobra egipcia
Egyptian cobra

la rana del dardo
poison dart frog

el tritón
newt

el sapo
toad

el caimán
alligator

el cocodrilo
crocodile

Peces • *Fish*

Los peces son animales acuáticos que viven y se reproducen en el agua; la mayoría tienen la piel recubierta de escamas y se desplazan por el agua utilizando sus aletas y su potente cuerpo y cola. Los peces respiran debajo del agua a través de las agallas, las cuales absorben el oxígeno que está disuelto en el agua.

Fish live and breed in water. Most fish are covered in scales, and they swim by using their fins and their powerful bodies and tails. Fish use gills to breathe under water. The gills take in the oxygen that is dissolved in water.

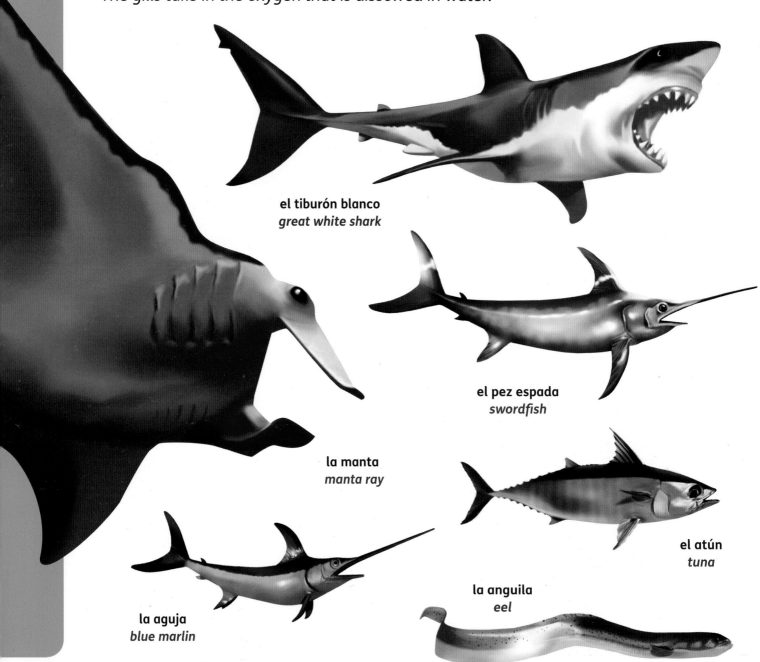

el tiburón blanco
great white shark

el pez espada
swordfish

la manta
manta ray

el atún
tuna

la aguja
blue marlin

la anguila
eel

Partes de un pez • *Parts of a fish*

la aleta
fin

las escamas
scales

la aleta caudal
tail fin

el opérculo
gill cover

la trucha • *trout*

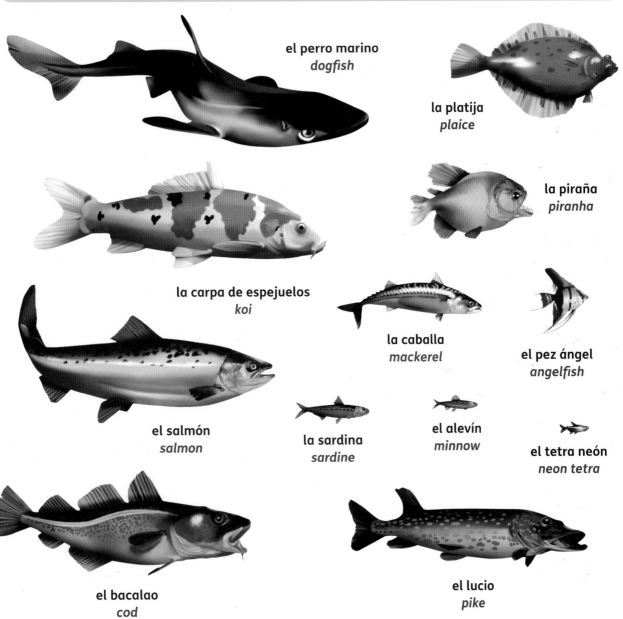

el perro marino
dogfish

la platija
plaice

la piraña
piranha

la carpa de espejuelos
koi

la caballa
mackerel

el pez ángel
angelfish

el salmón
salmon

la sardina
sardine

el alevín
minnow

el tetra neón
neon tetra

el bacalao
cod

el lucio
pike

Animales marinos
Sea creatures

A medida que nos sumergimos en el mar, nos vamos a encontrar con una gran variedad de animales marinos. Hay mamíferos (como las ballenas y los delfines), anfibios (como las tortugas de mar), reptiles marinos (como las serpientes de mar), y una gran diversidad de peces.

As you dive deep into the sea, you find an amazing range of creatures. There are mammals (such as whales and dolphins), amphibians (like turtles), marine reptiles (like sea snakes), and many varieties of fish.

1 el pez volador
flying fish

2 la anémona
anemone

3 la foca
seal

4 la ballena azul
blue whale

5 el pulpo dumbo
dumbo octopus

6 la langosta mantis
mantis shrimp

7 la araña de mar
sea spider

8 el delfín
dolphin

9 la morsa
walrus

10 la tortuga de mar
sea turtle

11 la serpiente de mar
sea snake

12 el pulpo
octopus

13 la langosta
lobster

14 el caballito de mar
seahorse

15 el nautilo
nautilus

16 el tiburón ballena
whale shark

17 el calamar gigante
giant squid

18 la medusa gigante
giant jellyfish

19 el tiburón boreal
Greenland shark

20 el pepino de mar
sea cucumber

21 el isópodo gigante
giant isopod

Animales y plantas

Insectos y bichos • *Insects and mini-beasts*

Los insectos tienen seis patas, no tienen columna vertebral, y tienen el cuerpo dividido en tres partes (la cabeza, el tórax y el abdomen). Otros insectos pequeños sin columna vertebral son las arañas, los ciempiés y los escarabajos. A estos insectos se les suele llamar bichos.

Insects have six legs, no backbone, and a body divided into three parts (the head, the thorax, and the abdomen). Other small creatures without a backbone include spiders, centipedes, and beetles. These creatures are often known as mini-beasts.

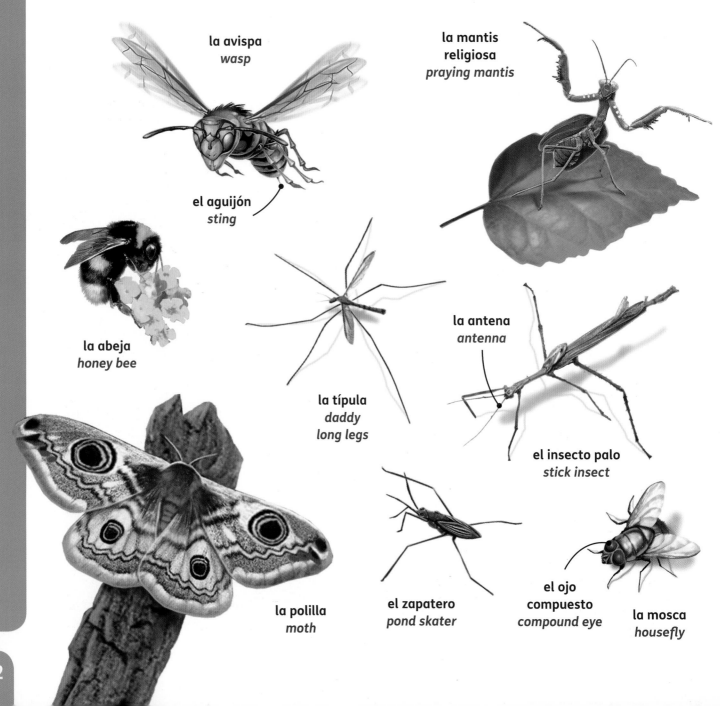

la avispa
wasp

la mantis religiosa
praying mantis

el aguijón
sting

la abeja
honey bee

la antena
antenna

la típula
daddy long legs

el insecto palo
stick insect

la polilla
moth

el zapatero
pond skater

el ojo compuesto
compound eye

la mosca
housefly

Animals and plants

la libélula
dragonfly

la tijereta
earwig

el chinche
bedbug

la cucaracha
cockroach

la pulga
flea

el mosquito
mosquito

la oruga
caterpillar

la mariposa
butterfly

la cabeza
head

el tórax
thorax

el abdomen
abdomen

la hormiga
ant

el áfido
aphid

la mariquita
ladybird

el saltamontes
grasshopper

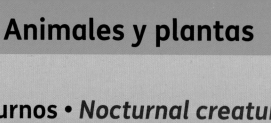

Animales nocturnos • *Nocturnal creatures*

Los animales nocturnos duermen o descansan durante el día y cazan durante la noche.

Nocturnal creatures sleep or rest during the day. They come out in the evening or at night to look for food.

1 el tejón • *badger*	**4** la babosa leopardo • *leopard slug*	**7** el escorpión • *scorpion*
2 la polilla luna • *moth*	**5** el lobo gris • *grey wolf*	**8** la mofeta • *skunk*
3 el lémur • *lemur*	**6** el erizo • *hedgehog*	**9** el vampiro • *bat*

Animals and plants

9

10

11

12

13

14

15

16

17

18

10 el mapache • *raccoon*

11 el lirón • *dormouse*

12 el tarsero • *tarsier*

13 el zorro • *fox*

14 el puercoespín • *porcupine*

15 el ermitaño • *hermit crab*

16 la zarigüeya • *possum*

17 el armadillo • *armadillo*

18 la lechuza • *barn owl*

Aves • *Birds*

Las aves tienen dos patas, dos alas, y un pico. Todas las aves ponen huevos y tienen el cuerpo cubierto de plumas. La mayoría de las aves pueden volar, pero hay algunas, como el pingüino, el emú, y el avestruz, que no pueden volar.

Birds have two legs, two wings, and a beak. All birds lay eggs and are covered with feathers. Most birds can fly, but there are some flightless birds, such as the penguin, the emu, and the ostrich.

el martín pescador
kingfisher

el petirrojo
robin

la golondrina
swallow

el pájaro carpintero
woodpecker

el cuco
cuckoo

la garza real
heron

el mirlo
blackbird

el pavo real
peacock

Exóticas y maravillosas • *Astonishing and amazing*

la espátula rosada
roseate spoonbill

el cálao de casco
helmeted hornbill

el ave fragata
frigate bird

el buitre
vulture

el águila
eagle

el avestruz
ostrich

el pelícano
pelican

el colibrí
hummingbird

el flamenco
flamingo

el pingüino
penguin

el frailecillo
puffin

Árboles y arbustos • *Trees and shrubs*

Los árboles son plantas muy grandes que tardan varios años en alcanzar su altura natural; tienen el tronco ancho y leñoso y las raíces muy profundas. Los arbustos son matas de tallo leñoso. Son arbustos algunas hierbas, como por ejemplo la lavanda, el romero y la salvia.

Trees are very large plants that take many years to grow to their full size. They have a thick and woody trunk and very deep roots. Shrubs are bushes with woody stems. They include some herbs, such as lavender, rosemary, and sage.

el pino
pine

el tejo
yew

el baobab
baobab

la secuoya
redwood

el abeto
fir

el castaño de Indias
horse chestnut

la palmera
palm

el roble
oak

el haya
beech

el acebo
holly

el olivo
olive

el cerezo
cherry

el manzano
apple

el limonero
lemon

la mimosa
mimosa

el romero
rosemary

la lavanda
lavender

Partes de un árbol
Parts of a tree

las hojas
leaves

las ramas
branch

el tronco
trunk

la raíz
root

la corteza
bark

el sicomoro • *sycamore*

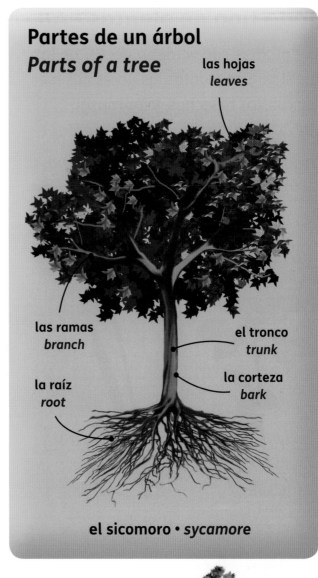

el eucalipto
eucalyptus

Todo tipo de plantas • *All sorts of plants*

Las plantas son verdes y necesitan luz para crecer. Hay muchos tipos distintos de plantas. Son plantas las flores, las hierbas aromáticas, las plantas herbáceas, los cactus, los helechos, y los musgos.

Plants are green and need light to grow. There are many different types of plant, including flowering plants, herbs, grasses, cacti, ferns, and mosses.

la rosa
rose

el narciso
daffodil

el tulipán
tulip

el pensamiento
pansy

el lirio
lily

la orquídea
orchid

el girasol
sunflower

la amapola
poppy

el nenúfar
water lily

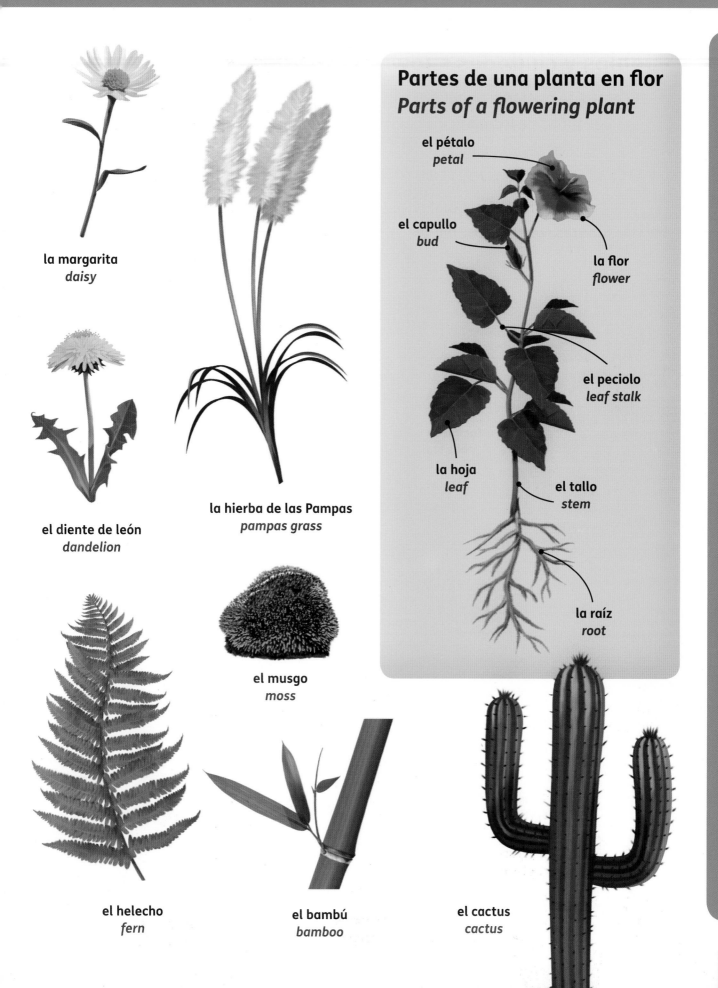

la margarita
daisy

el diente de león
dandelion

la hierba de las Pampas
pampas grass

el helecho
fern

el musgo
moss

el bambú
bamboo

el cactus
cactus

Partes de una planta en flor
Parts of a flowering plant

el pétalo
petal

el capullo
bud

la flor
flower

el peciolo
leaf stalk

la hoja
leaf

el tallo
stem

la raíz
root

Pueblos y ciudades • *Towns and cities*

En el centro de nuestros pueblos y ciudades hay oficinas, museos y bancos y algunos de los edificios más grandes del mundo; en las afueras están los barrios residenciales, donde vive la mayoría de la gente.

In the centre of our towns and cities are offices, museums, and banks. They are some of the largest buildings in the world. On the outskirts are the suburbs, where most people live.

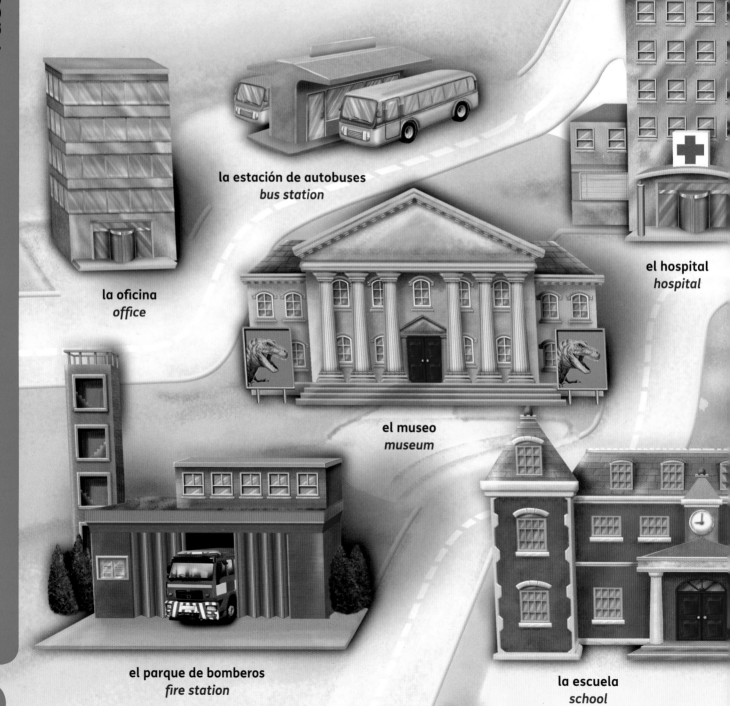

la estación de autobuses
bus station

la oficina
office

el hospital
hospital

el museo
museum

el parque de bomberos
fire station

la escuela
school

el parking
car park

el estadio
stadium

el supermercado
supermarket

el hotel
hotel

el restaurante
restaurant

el ayuntamiento
city hall

el cine
cinema

Towns and cities

En la calle • *On the street*

Las calles de las ciudades pueden ser muy bulliciosas, ya que en ellas hay muchas tiendas, negocios y cafés. Algunas calles son peatonales y así es más agradable ir de compras y salir con los amigos.

City streets can be very lively places. They are full of shops, businesses, and cafes. In some streets, most traffic is banned so the pedestrians can enjoy shopping and meeting friends.

1 el café
cafe

2 el quiosco
news stand

3 la tienda
convenience store

4 el banco
bank

5 la oficina de correos
post office

6 el buzón
post box

7 la parada de autobús
bus stop

8 la calle
road

9 la acera
pavement

10 la farola
street light

11 el parquímetro
parking meter

12 la papelera
litter bin

13 la frutería
greengrocer

14 la librería
book shop

Todo tipo de tiendas • *All sorts of shops*

la juguetería
toy shop

la panadería
baker

la carnicería
butcher

la farmacia
chemist

la tienda de ropa
clothes shop

la tienda de golosinas
sweet shop

la floristería
florist

la tienda de regalos
gift shop

la tienda de periódicos
newsagent

la pajarería
pet shop

la zapatería
shoe shop

En el campo • *In the country*

En todas las partes del mundo, se trabaja el campo y se crían animales. Los agricultores cultivan productos agrícolas y los ganaderos crían vacas lecheras o cabras para obtener su leche, que a veces se transforma en queso, mantequilla, o en otros productos lácteos.

All over the world, people farm the land and raise animals in the countryside. Arable farmers grow crops. Dairy farmers keep cows or goats for their milk. Milk is sometimes turned into cheese, butter, or other dairy products.

Cultivos y hortalizas • *Crops and vegetables*

la caña de azúcar • *sugar cane*

la soja • *soybeans*

el maíz • *maize*

el trigo • *wheat*

las calabazas • *pumpkins*

las patatas • *potatoes*

el arroz • *rice*

las uvas • *grapes*

Vehículos y máquinas agrícolas • *Farm vehicles and machinery*

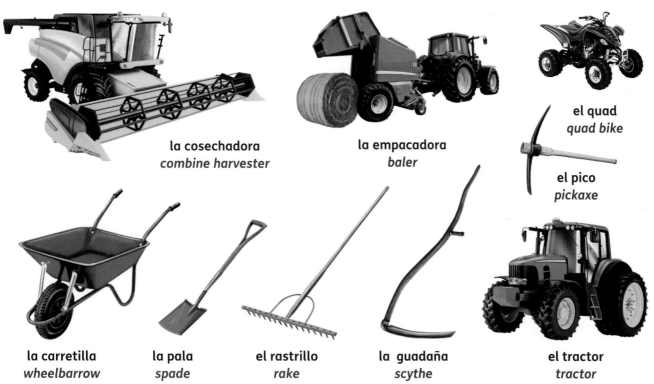

la cosechadora
combine harvester

la empacadora
baler

el quad
quad bike

el pico
pickaxe

la carretilla
wheelbarrow

la pala
spade

el rastrillo
rake

la guadaña
scythe

el tractor
tractor

Edificios de la granja • *Farm buildings*

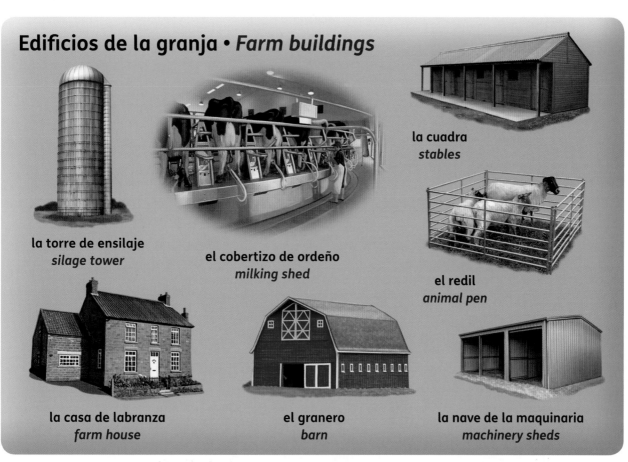

la torre de ensilaje
silage tower

el cobertizo de ordeño
milking shed

la cuadra
stables

el redil
animal pen

la casa de labranza
farm house

el granero
barn

la nave de la maquinaria
machinery sheds

Paisajes y hábitats • *Landscapes and habitats*

En la Tierra hay muchos tipos de paisajes. Cada paisaje facilita un hábitat especial para un tipo distinto de fauna y flora. Los paisajes varían desde hielo muy espeso y nieve en el polo Norte y en el polo Sur hasta selvas tropicales húmedas cerca del ecuador.

The Earth has many different types of landscape, and each landscape provides a special habitat for a different set of wildlife. Landscapes can range from thick ice and snow around the North and South poles to steamy rainforests close to the equator.

el océano
ocean

la orilla del mar
seashore

la montaña
mountain

la selva tropical
rainforest

el desierto
desert

las praderas
grasslands

el glaciar
glacier

el bosque de hoja perenne
evergreen forest

el bosque
woodland

el lago
lake

la región polar
polar region

la zona pantanosa
swamp

el brezal
moor

Etapas de un río
Stages of a river

Los ríos proporcionan un hábitat muy cambiante para la fauna y la flora: en su nacimiento son arroyos de escaso caudal y de corriente rápida, y en la desembocadura son ríos anchos y de corriente lenta.

Rivers provide a changing habitat for wildlife, starting with a tiny, fast-flowing stream, and ending in a broad, slow-moving river.

el arroyo
stream

el afluente
tributary

los rápidos
rapids

la cascada
waterfall

el estuario
estuary

Landscapes and habitats

99

El tiempo • *Weather*

Los lugares próximos al ecuador tienen clima tropical; el tiempo en esta zona es caluroso y húmedo durante todo el año. En los lugares situados más al norte y al sur el clima es templado y se caracteriza por ser frío en invierno, más suave en primavera y otoño, y cálido en verano.

Places close to the Equator have a tropical climate. The weather there is hot and humid all year round. In places further north and south, the climate is temperate. It is cold in the winter, cool in spring and autumn, and warm in summer.

soleado • *sunny*

nublado • *cloudy*

lluvioso • *rainy*

de niebla • *foggy*

de neblina tóxica • *smoggy*

de nieve • *snowy*

glacial • *icy*

el vendaval de polvo • *dust storm*

la granizada • *hailstorm*

la tormenta • *thunderstorm*

Para hablar de temperaturas
Temperature words

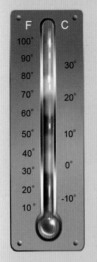

F	C	
100°		**caluroso** *hot*
90°	30°	
80°		**cálido** *warm*
70°	20°	
60°		**fresco** *cool*
50°	10°	
40°		
30°	0°	**frío** *cold*
20°		
10°	-10°	**bajo cero** *freezing*

el clima tropical
tropical climate

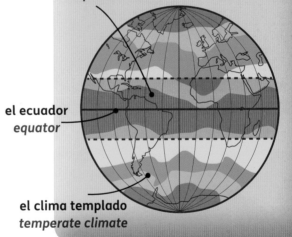

el ecuador
equator

el clima templado
temperate climate

el tornado • *tornado*

Contaminación y conservación
Pollution and conservation

La Tierra se encuentra amenazada por contaminación de varios tipos. También estamos corriendo el riesgo de agotar los recursos energéticos de la Tierra. Si queremos salvar nuestro planeta, tenemos que reducir la contaminación y ahorrar energía.

Planet Earth is threatened by many kinds of pollution. We are also in danger of using up the Earth's resources of energy. If we want to save our planet, we must reduce pollution and conserve (save) energy.

Tipos de contaminación
Types of pollution

los desechos peligrosos
hazardous waste

la contaminación de las aguas
water contamination

la contaminación atmosférica
air pollution

la intoxicación por pesticidas
pesticide poisoning

la radiación
radiation

la contaminación acústica
noise pollution

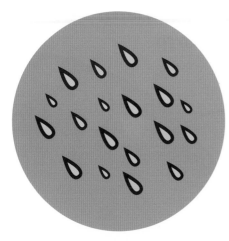

la lluvia ácida
acid rain

el vertido de petróleo
oil spill

la contaminación
lumínica
light pollution

Ahorro de energía • *Energy conservation*

Podemos tomar varias medidas para ayudar a ahorrar energía y mantener nuestro planeta en buen estado.

People can take a range of steps to help save energy and keep the planet healthy.

el abono orgánico
composting

la reutilización
re-use

el ahorro de energía
energy saving

el reciclaje
recycling

La Tierra
Planet Earth

Los seres humanos viven en la superficie de la corteza terrestre, y esta corteza tiene forma de diferentes paisajes. Debajo de la corteza hay varias capas de roca, y algunas están fundidas (a temperaturas muy altas y líquidas). Los volcanes entran en erupción cuando la roca fundida, llamada lava, es expulsada a la superficie de la Tierra de forma violenta.

Humans live on the surface crust of the Earth, and this crust is moulded into different landscape features. Underneath the crust are several layers of rock, and some of them are molten (very hot and liquid). Volcanoes erupt when molten rock, called lava, bursts through the Earth's crust.

Topografía del paisaje
Landscape features

El interior de la Tierra
Inside the Earth

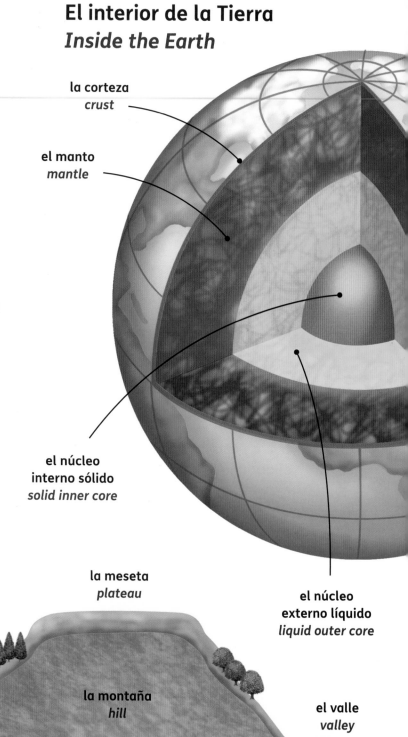

la corteza
crust

el manto
mantle

el núcleo interno sólido
solid inner core

el núcleo externo líquido
liquid outer core

la meseta
plateau

la montaña
hill

el valle
valley

la llanura
plain

El interior de un volcán
Inside a volcano

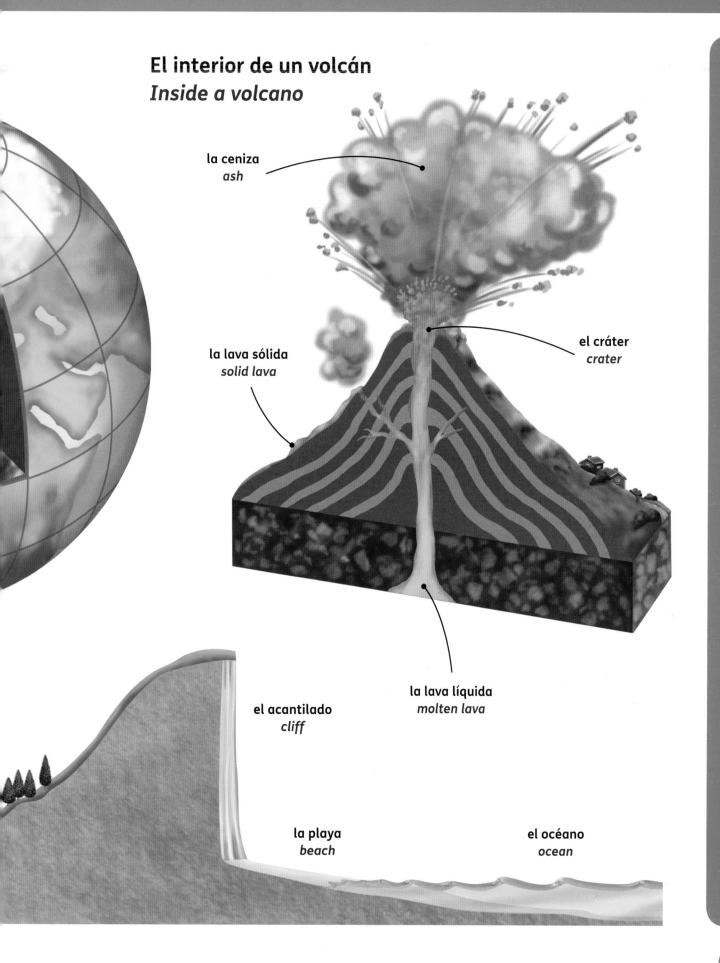

la ceniza
ash

el cráter
crater

la lava sólida
solid lava

la lava líquida
molten lava

el acantilado
cliff

la playa
beach

el océano
ocean

El sistema solar

El sistema solar
The solar system

Nuestro sistema solar está compuesto por el Sol y los planetas que giran a su alrededor. En nuestro sistema solar hay ocho planetas y muchas lunas. También hay muchos asteroides y cometas que giran alrededor del Sol.

Our solar system is made up of the Sun and the planets that orbit it. In our solar system, there are eight planets and many moons. There are also many asteroids and comets that orbit the Sun.

el Sol
Sun

Mercurio
Mercury

Venus
Venus

la Tierra
Earth

Marte
Mars

Júpiter
Jupiter

Palabras de astronomía • *Space words*

La gente utiliza los telescopios para estudiar el cielo por la noche. Los observadores de estrellas profesionales se llaman astrónomos.

People use telescopes to study the sky at night. Professional stargazers are called astronomers.

la estrella • *star*

la constelación • *constellation*

la luna • *moon*

la Vía Láctea • *Milky Way*

la galaxia • *galaxy*

el meteoro • *meteor*

el agujero negro • *black hole*

Saturno
Saturn

Urano
Uranus

Neptuno
Neptune

Viajes espaciales • *Space travel*

El hombre lleva explorando el espacio desde hace más de 50 años. Cohetes potentes lanzan al espacio transbordadores espaciales y otras naves espaciales. Las sondas y las estaciones espaciales investigan el espacio, y los robots exploradores y los módulos de aterrizaje exploran otros planetas. Algunas naves espaciales van tripuladas por astronautas, pero muchas son controladas por robots.

Humans have been exploring space for over 50 years. Powerful rockets launch space shuttles and other spacecraft into space. Probes and space stations investigate space, and rovers and landers explore other planets. Some spacecraft carry astronauts, but many are operated by robots.

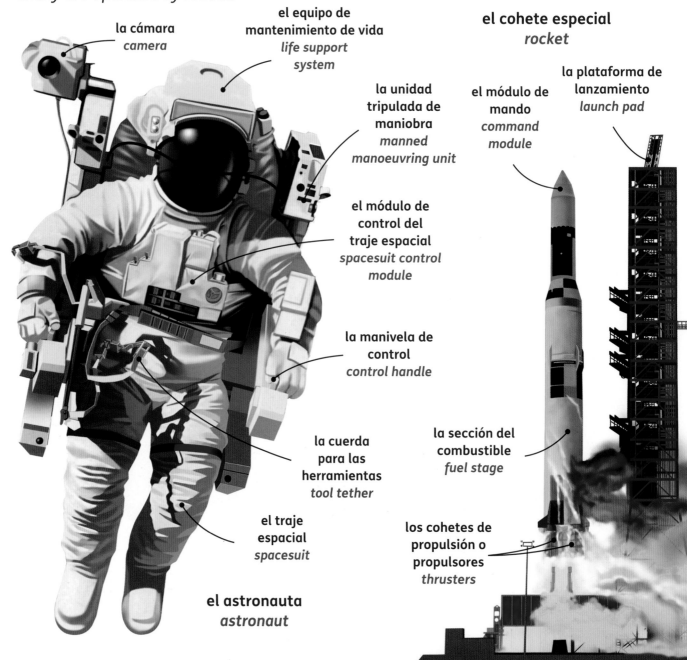

la cámara
camera

el equipo de mantenimiento de vida
life support system

el cohete especial
rocket

la unidad tripulada de maniobra
manned manoeuvring unit

el módulo de mando
command module

la plataforma de lanzamiento
launch pad

el módulo de control del traje espacial
spacesuit control module

la manivela de control
control handle

la cuerda para las herramientas
tool tether

la sección del combustible
fuel stage

el traje espacial
spacesuit

los cohetes de propulsión o propulsores
thrusters

el astronauta
astronaut

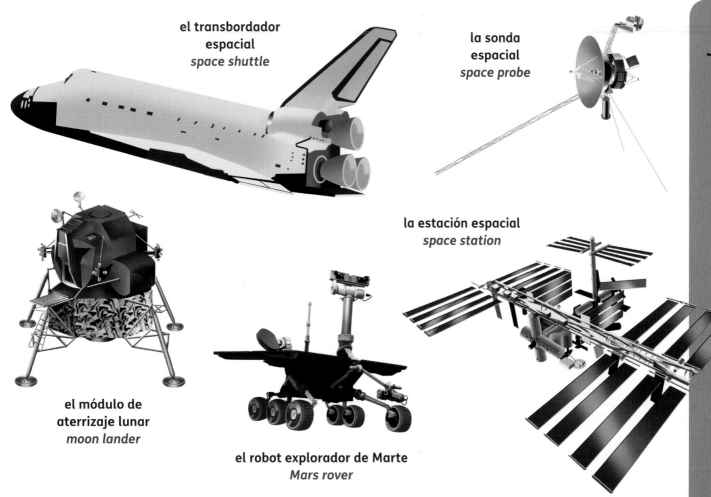

el transbordador espacial
space shuttle

la sonda espacial
space probe

la estación espacial
space station

el módulo de aterrizaje lunar
moon lander

el robot explorador de Marte
Mars rover

Satélites • *Satellites*

Los satélites giran alrededor de la Tierra. Se utilizan para sacar fotografías, retransmitir mensajes y para el seguimiento meteorológico.

Satellites orbit the Earth. They are used to take photographs, to transmit messages, and to track the weather.

satélite de observación de la Tierra
Earth observation satellite

satélite meteorológico
weather satellite

satélite de comunicaciones
communications satellite

Los números • *Numbers*

0	cero • *zero*	
1	uno • *one*	
2	dos • *two*	
3	tres • *three*	
4	cuatro • *four*	
5	cinco • *five*	
6	seis • *six*	
7	siete • *seven*	
8	ocho • *eight*	
9	nueve • *nine*	
10	diez • *ten*	
11	once • *eleven*	
12	doce • *twelve*	
13	trece • *thirteen*	
14	catorce • *fourteen*	
15	quince • *fifteen*	
16	dieciséis • *sixteen*	
17	diecisiete • *seventeen*	
18	dieciocho • *eighteen*	
19	diecinueve • *nineteen*	
20	veinte • *twenty*	
21	veintiuno • *twenty-one*	
22	veintidós • *twenty-two*	
23	veintitrés • *twenty-three*	
24	veinticuatro • *twenty-four*	
25	veinticinco • *twenty-five*	
30	treinta • *thirty*	

40 cuarenta • *forty*

50 cincuenta • *fifty*

60 sesenta • *sixty*

70 setenta • *seventy*

80 ochenta • *eighty*

90 noventa • *ninety*

100 cien • *a hundred, one hundred*

101 ciento uno • *a hundred and one, one hundred and one*

1,000
mil • *a thousand, one thousand*

10,000
diez mil • *ten thousand*

1,000,000
un millón • *a million, one million*

1,000,000,000
mil millones • *a billion, one billion*

1º primero, primera • *first*

2º segundo, segunda • *second*

3º tercero, tercera • *third*

4º cuarto, cuarta • *fourth*

5º quinto, quinta • *fifth*

6º sexto, sexta • *sixth*

7º séptimo, séptima • *seventh*

8º octavo, octava • *eighth*

9º noveno, novena • *ninth*

10º décimo, décima • *tenth*

11º undécimo, undécima • *eleventh*

12º duodécimo, duodécima • *twelfth*

13º decimotercero, decimotercera *thirteenth*

14º decimocuarto, decimocuarta *fourteenth*

15º decimoquinto, decimoquinta *fifteenth*

16⁰	**decimosexto, decimosexta** *sixteenth*
17⁰	**decimoséptimo, decimoséptima** *seventeenth*
18⁰	**decimoctavo, decimoctava** *eighteenth*
19⁰	**decimonoveno, decimonovena** *nineteenth*
20⁰	**vigésimo, vigésima** *twentieth*
21⁰	**vigesimoprimero, vigesimoprimera** *twenty-first*
30⁰	**trigésimo, trigésima** *thirtieth*
40⁰	**cuadragésimo, cuadragésima** *fortieth*
50⁰	**quincuagésimo, quincuagésima** *fiftieth*
60⁰	**sexagésimo, sexagésima** *sixtieth*
70⁰	**septuagésimo, septuagésima** *seventieth*
80⁰	**octogésimo, octogésima** *eightieth*
90⁰	**nonagésimo, nonagésima** *ninetieth*
100⁰	**centésimo, centésima** *one hundredth*
1,000⁰	**milésimo, milésima** *one thousandth*

Las fracciones
Fractions

una mitad • *half*
un tercio • *third*
una cuarta parte • *quarter*
una octava parte • *eighth*

Las medidas
Measurements

milímetro • *millimetre*
centímetro • *centimetre*
metro • *metre*
kilómetro • *kilometre*
gramo • *gram*
kilogramo • *kilogram*
tonelada • *tonne*
mililitro • *millilitre*
centilitro • *centilitre*
litro • *litre*
grado Celcius • *celsius*
grado centígrado • *centigrade*

la altura • *height*
la profundidad • *depth*
el ancho • *width*
la longitud • *length*

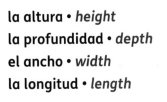

Operaciones aritméticas
Maths words

multiplicar • *multiply*
sumar • *add*
restar • *subtract*
dividir • *divide*

Los días de la semana
Days of the week

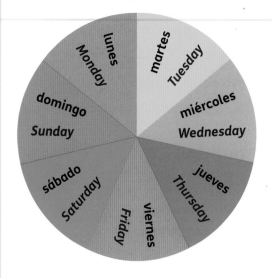

lunes Monday
martes Tuesday
miércoles Wednesday
jueves Thursday
viernes Friday
sábado Saturday
domingo Sunday

Los meses
Months

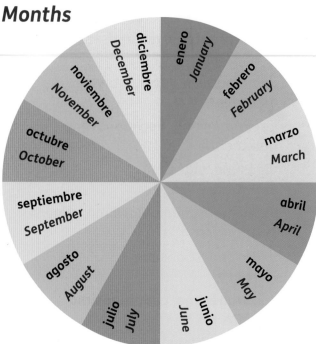

enero January
febrero February
marzo March
abril April
mayo May
junio June
julio July
agosto August
septiembre September
octubre October
noviembre November
diciembre December

Las estaciones • Seasons

la primavera
spring

el verano
summer

el otoño
autumn

el invierno
winter

Palabras de tiempo • Time words

el milenio millennium	**el siglo** century	**el año** year
el mes month	**la semana** week	**el día** day
la hora hour	**el minuto** minute	**el segundo** second

Momentos del día • Times of day

el amanecer dawn	**la mañana** morning	**el mediodía** midday	**la tarde** afternoon
la tarde evening	**la noche** night	**la medianoche** midnight	

La hora • *Telling the time*

las nueve
nine o'clock

las nueve y cinco
five past nine

las nueve y diez
nine ten,
ten past nine

las nueve y cuarto
nine fifteen,
quarter past nine

las nueve y veinte
nine twenty,
twenty past nine

las nueve y veinticinco
nine twenty-five,
twenty-five past nine

las nueve y media
nine thirty,
half past nine

las nueve treinta y cinco,
las diez menos veinticinco
nine thirty-five,
twenty-five to ten

las nueve y cuarenta,
las diez menos veinte
nine forty,
twenty to ten

las nueve y cuarenta
y cinco, las diez
menos cuarto
nine forty-five,
quarter to ten

las nueve y cincuenta,
las diez menos diez
nine fifty,
ten to ten

las nueve y
cincuenta y cinco,
las diez menos cinco
nine fifty-five,
five to ten

Los colores • *Colours*

negro
black

rojo
red

azul
blue

verde
green

amarillo
yellow

gris
grey

naranja
orange

marrón
brown

rosa
pink

morado
purple

blanco
white

Las formas • *Shapes*

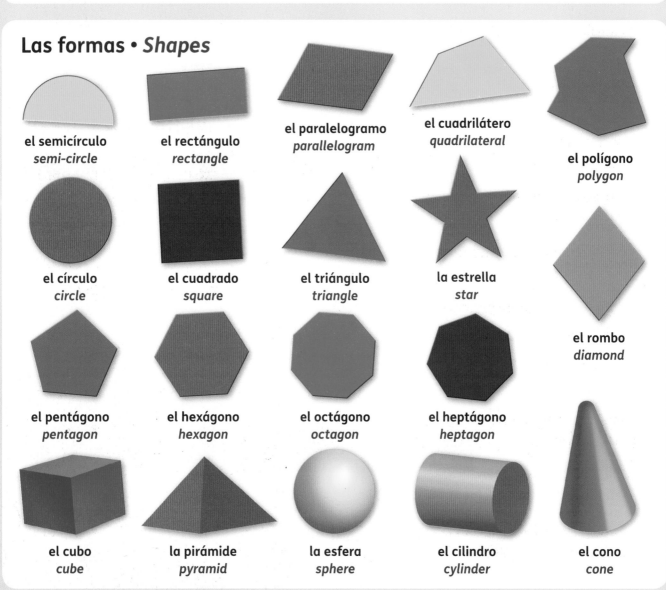

el semicírculo
semi-circle

el rectángulo
rectangle

el paralelogramo
parallelogram

el cuadrilátero
quadrilateral

el polígono
polygon

el círculo
circle

el cuadrado
square

el triángulo
triangle

la estrella
star

el rombo
diamond

el pentágono
pentagon

el hexágono
hexagon

el octágono
octagon

el heptágono
heptagon

el cubo
cube

la pirámide
pyramid

la esfera
sphere

el cilindro
cylinder

el cono
cone

Opuestos
Opposites

grande – pequeño/pequeña
big – small

limpio/limpia – sucio/sucia
clean – dirty

gordo/gorda – delgado/delgada
fat – thin

lleno/llena – vacío/vacía
full – empty

alto/alta – bajo/baja
high – low

caliente – frío/fría
hot – cold

abierto/abierta – cerrado/cerrada
open – closed

pesado/pesada – ligero/ligera
heavy – light

fuerte – silencioso/silenciosa
loud – quiet

duro/dura – blando/blanda
hard – soft

largo/larga – corto/corta
long – short

claro/clara – oscuro/oscura
light – dark

seco/seca – mojado/mojada
dry – wet

rápido/rápida – lento/lenta
fast – slow

Palabras de posición
Position words

en *on*	**de** *off*
debajo de *under*	**encima de, sobre** *over*
al lado de *next to*	**entre** *between*
encima *above*	**debajo** *below*
delante de *in front of*	**detrás de** *behind*
lejos *far*	**cerca** *near*

Índice español • *Spanish index*

¡hacia arriba! **55**
abanico *(m)* 30
abdomen *(m)* 83
abeja *(f)* 82
abeto *(m)* 88
abogado, abogada *(m/f)* 35
abono orgánico *(m)* 103
absorbente 65
abuela *(f)* 10
abuelo *(m)* 10
aburrido 17
acantilado *(m)* 105
acebo *(m)* 89
acera *(f)* 94
acero *(m)* 65
ácido 16
actor, actriz *(m/f)* 50
acuarelas *(pl)* 45
aerodeslizador *(m)* 61
aeronaves *(pl)* **58**
áfido *(m)* 83
afluente *(m)* 99
agente de policía *(m/f)* 35
agradable 16
agua *(m)* 22
aguacates *(pl)* 26
aguijón *(m)* 82
águila *(m)* 87
aguja *(f)* 67, 78
agujero negro *(m)* 107
ahorro de energía *(m)* **103**
ala *(m)* 58, 59
ala delta *(m)* 59
albañil *(m)* **37**
albóndigas *(pl)* 24
alegre 17
aleta *(f)* 36, 79
aleta caudal *(f)* 79
alevín *(m)* 79
algodón *(m)* 21, 64
amapola *(f)* 90
ambulancia *(f)* 57
amigos *(pl)* 11
ancas de rana *(pl)* 25
ancla *(m)* 61
anémona *(f)* 80
anguila *(f)* 78
animales domésticos *(pl)* **74**
animales marinos *(pl)* **80**
animales nocturnos *(pl)* **84**
animales pequeños *(pl)* **75**
antena *(f)* 82
antena de radio *(f)* 67
antena parabólica *(f)* 66

apagado 65
apisonadora *(f)* 56
araña de mar *(f)* 80
árbitro *(m)* 39
árboles y arbustos *(pl)* **88**
archivar 71
archivo adjunto *(m)* 70
arcilla de modelar *(f)* 45
arco *(m)* 47
ardilla *(f)* 73
armadillo *(m)* 85
armadura *(f)* 30
armario del cuarto de baño *(m)*
    21
arpa *(m)* 47
arquitecto, arquitecta *(m/f)* 34
arrastrar 71
arroyo *(m)* 99
arroz *(m)* 23, 96
**artes plásticas y
    manualidades** *(pl)* **44**
artículos de la casa *(pl)* **20**
áspero 65
astronauta *(m)* 108
asustado 17
atacar 40
atletismo *(m)* 38
atún *(m)* 78
autocar *(f)* 55
autocaravana *(f)* 54
ave fragata *(m)* 87
aves *(pl)* **86**
avestruz *(m)* 87
avión de pasajeros *(m)* 59
avión ultraligero *(m)* 59
avispa *(f)* 82
ayuntamiento *(m)* 93
babosa leopardo *(f)* 84
bacalao *(m)* 79
bagala *(f)* 61
bailarín, bailarina *(m/f)* 50
baile *(m)* **49**
baile de salón *(m)* 49
bajar 70
bajo cero 101
balcón *(m)* 67
ballena azul *(f)* 80
ballet *(m)* 49
balón *(m)* 42
baloncesto *(m)* 39
bambú *(m)* 91
banco *(m)* 94
bañera *(f)* 19
baobab *(m)* 88

barbilla *(f)* 12
barquilla *(f)* 59
barra de control *(f)* 58
barriga *(f)* 13
bata quirúrgica *(f)* 36
bate *(m)* 42
batería *(f)* 47
bebidas *(pl)* 22
bebidas con gas *(pl)* 22
béisbol *(m)* 38
bicicleta *(f)* 55
biplano *(m)* 59
bisabuela *(f)* 10
bisabuelo *(m)* 10
bisturí *(m)* 36
blando 65
bloc de dibujo *(m)* 45
bloc de notas *(m)* 33
blog *(m)* 70
blusa *(f)* 31
boca *(f)* 12
bocadillo *(m)* 24
bodegón *(m)* 44
bolas de malabares *(pl)* 42
bolígrafo *(m)* 33
bollo *(m)* 24
bolsa *(f)* 59
bombera *(f)* **37**
borrar 71
bosque *(m)* 98
bosque de hoja perenne *(m)* ... 98
botas de fútbol *(pl)* 29
botas incombustibles *(pl)* 37
botavara *(f)* 60
bote de remos *(m)* 61
botella de aire comprimido *(f)* 36
botines *(pl)* 29
brazo *(m)* 13
breakdance *(m)* 49
brezal *(m)* 99
brillante 16, 65
bronce *(m)* 65
búfalo de agua *(m)* 74
bufanda *(f)* 29
buitre *(m)* 87
buque cisterna *(m)* 60
**buques, barcos y otras
    embarcaciones** **60**
burro *(m)* 75
buscar 70
buzo *(m)* **36**
buzón *(m)* 94
caballa *(f)* 79
caballero medieval *(m)* 30

caballito de mar *(m)* 80
caballo *(m)* 74
cabeza *(f)* 13, 83
cabina de piloto *(f)* 59
cable principal *(m)* 67
cable tirante *(m)* 67
cabra *(f)* 74
cacerola *(f)* 20
cactus *(m)* 91
cadera *(f)* 14
café *(m)* 22, 94
cager 41
caimán *(m)* 77
calabazas *(pl)* 26, 96
calamar gigante *(m)* 80
cálao de casco *(m)* 87
calcetines *(pl)* 29
calculadora *(f)* 33
cálido 101
caliente 16
calle *(f)* 94
caluroso 101
cama *(f)* 19
camaleón *(m)* 76
cámara *(f)* 50, 108
cámara *(m)* 50
cámara digital *(m)* 71
camello *(m)* 72
camión hormigonera *(m)* 57
camión portacoches *(m)* 57
camión portacontenedores *(m)*
    57
camión volquete *(m)* 56
camisa *(f)* 28
camiseta *(f)* 29
caña de azúcar *(f)* 96
canguro *(m)* 73
canoa *(f)* 61
cantante *(m/f)* 50
capa *(f)* 30
capó *(m)* 54
capullo *(m)* 91
cara *(f)* 12
caramelos *(pl)* 23
carbón *(m)* 63
carboncillo *(m)* 45
carga *(f)* 69
carne *(f)* 23
carnicería *(f)* 95
carpa de espejuelos *(f)* 79
carpeta de anillas *(f)* 33
carretilla *(f)* 97
carretilla elevadora *(f)* 56
casa *(f)* **18**

Índice español • *Spanish index*

casa de labranza (f) 97
cascada (f) 99
casco (m) 37, 58
casco de seguridad (m) 37
casita en el campo (f) 18
castaño de Indias (m) 88
castillo (m) 66
catamarán (m) 61
caucho (m) 64
cebolla (f) 26
cebra (f) 73
ceja (f) 12
ceniza (f) 105
cepillo de dientes (m) 21
cera (f) 64
cerebro (m) 15
cerezas (pl) 27
cerezo (m) 89
cerrar sesión 71
chalé (m) 18
chaleco (m) 31
champú (m) 21
chaqueta (f) 29, 31
chaqueta de chándal (f) 29
chaqueta de punto (f) 28
chat (m) 70
chelo (m) 47
chimenea (f) 19, 61
chinche (m) 83
chocolate (m) 23
chocolate a la taza (m) 22
ciclismo (m) 38
ciencias 33
ciervo (m) 73
cine (m) 93
cinta del pelo (f) 28
cinturón de herramientas (m) .. 37
cinturón de pesas (m) 36
cirujana (f) **36**
claqué (m) 49
claqueta (f) 50
clarinete (m) 46
clases (pl) **33**
clavícula (f) 14
clima templado (m) 101
clima tropical (m) 101
cobertizo de ordeño (m) 97
cobra egipcia (f) 77
cobre (m) 65
coche de bomberos (m)............ 57
coche deportivo (m).................. 54
coche familiar (m) 54
coche patrulla (m) 57
cocina (f) 19

cocina eléctrica/de gas (f)........ 19
cocodrilo (m) 77
codo (m) 13
cohete espacial (m) 108
cohetes de propulsión o
   propulsores (pl) 108
colador (m) 20
colibrí (m) 87
colores (pl) **114**
columna (f) 14, 67
comedia (f) 52
comida rápida **24**
Comida y bebidas **22**
conductor de autobús,
conductora de autobús (m/f).. 34
conectar 70, 71
conejillo de Indias (m) 75
confuso 17
constelación (f) 107
contaminación acústica (f)....102
contaminación atmosférica (f)
  102
contaminación de las aguas (f)
  102
contaminación lumínica (f) ...103
contaminación y conservación
   ....**102**
contrabajo (m) 47
copos de avena (pl) 23
coraza (f) 30
corazón (m) 15
corbata (f) 31
cordero (m) 24
corona (f) 30
correo electrónico (m)............. 70
cortar 71
corteza (f) 89, 104
cosechadora (f) 97
costillas (pl) 14
cráneo (m) 14
cráter (m) 105
crepes (pl) 25
criquet (m) 39
cristal (m) 64
cuaderno (m) 33
cuadra (f) 97
cuarto de baño (m) 19
cubierta (f) 61
cucaracha (f) 83
cuchara (f) 20
cucharón (m) 20
cuchillo (m) 20
cuco (m) 86
cuello (m) 13

cuerda (f) 69
cuerda para las herramientas (f)
  108
cuerpo (m) **12**
cuerpo humano (m) **13**
cultivos y hortalizas (pl) **96**
cúpula (f) 67
curry (m) 24
dar una patada a 40
de neblina tóxica 100
de niebla 100
de nieve 100
deberes (pl) 33
decorado (m) 50
dedos (pl) 13
dedos de los pies (pl) 13
defensa (m/f) 39
delantal (m) 31
delantero, delantera (m/f) 39
delfín (m) 80
deporte **38**
deporte en acción **40**
desechos peligrosos (pl) 102
desierto (m) 98
desilzarse 41
desplazarse 71
destornillador (m) 37
diagrama de un circuito
   eléctrico (f) **63**
días de la semana (pl) **112**
dibujo..................................... 33
dibujos animados (pl)..........44, 53
diente de león (m) 91
dientes (pl) 12
director (m) 50
director de escena, directora
   de escena (m/f) 50
disparar 41
documental de la naturaleza (m)
   53
dormitorio (m) 19
dragón de Kómodo (m) 76
ducha (m) 19
dulce 16
duro 65
DVD (m) 42
ecuador (m) 101
edificios de la granja (pl) **97**
edificios y estructuras (pl)...... **66**
editar 71
eje (m) 69
elefante (m) 72
empacadora (f) 97
emperatriz japonesa (f) 30

empujar 68
en el campo............................ **96**
en el cuarto de baño **21**
en Internet **70**
en la calle **94**
en la cocina **20**
en la escuela **32**
en tu cuerpo (m) **14**
energía **62**
energía de biomasa (f)............. 62
energía de las mareas (f) 62
energía eólica (f) 62
energía geotérmica (f) 62
energía hidroeléctrica (f).......... 62
energía nuclear (f) 63
energía solar (f) 62
enfadado 17
enfermero, enfermera (m/f) 35
ensalada (f) 25
entusiasmado 17
equipo de mantenimientode
   vida (m)..............................**108**
equipo de respiración (m) 37
equipo y ropa de trabajo 36
ereader (m) 71
erizo (m) 84
ermitaño (m) 85
esbozo (m) 44
escamas (pl) 79
escanear 71
escenario (m) 50
escorpión (m) 84
escuela (f) 92
escultura (f) 45
esnórkel (m) 36
espaguetis (pl) 25
espalda (f) 13
espátula (f) 20
espátula rosada (f) 87
espinilla (f) 14
esponja (f) 21
esqueleto (m)......................... **14**
estabilizador vertical (m).......... 59
estación de autobuses (f)......... 92
estación espacial (f) 109
estaciones (pl) **112**
estadio (m) 93
esternón (m) 14
estómago (m) 15
estrella (f) 107
estuario (m) 99
etapas de un río (pl)............... **99**
eucalipto (m) 89
examen (m) 33

Índice español • Spanish index

excavadora (f) 56
exóticas y maravillosas........... **86**
explorar.................... 70
falda (f) 29
falda escocesa (f) 31
familia (f) y amigos (pl)........... **10**
farmacia (f) 95
faro (m) 54
farola (f) 94
feliz 17
fémur (m) 14
ferry (m) 60
filete (m) 24
flamenco (m)................. 87
flauta (f) 46
flor (f) 91
floristería (f) 95
flotador (m) 58
foca (f) 80
foco (m) 50
formas (pl) **114**
formatear 71
fotografía (f) 44
fracciones (pl) **111**
frailecillo (m)................ 87
fregadero (m) 19
frente (f) 12
fresas (pl) 26
fresco 101
fricción.................... 68
frío 16, 101
fruta (f) 23
frutas y verduras (pl) **26**
frutería (f) 94
fuerte 16
fuerzas en acción 68
fuerzas y máquinas (pl) **68**
fulcro (m)................. **69**
funicular (m) 55
furgoneta de reparto (f)....... 57
fútbol (m) **38, 39**
galaxia (f) 107
gallina (f) 75
gallo (m) 75
ganso (m) 75
garaje (m) 19
garza real (f) 86
gas natural (m) 63
gato (m) 75
gel de ducha (m) 21
geografía 33
gimnasia (f) 38
girafa (f) 72
girasol (m) 90

glacial 101
glaciar (m) 98
globo (m) 33
globo aerostático (m) 59
gol (m) 39
golf (m).................... 39
golondrina (f)................ 86
golpear 40
goma (f) 33
gorila (m) 73
gorra (f) 28
gorro (m) 29, 36
grafiti (m).................. 45
granero (m) 97
granizada (f)................101
grapadora (f)................ 33
gravedad................... 68
grúa con cesta (f) 56
grúa mecánica (f) 56
guadaña (f) 97
guantelete (m) 30
guantes (pl) 29
guardar 71
guepardo (m) 73
guerrero samurái del Japón (m)
   30
guisantes (pl) 26
guitarra (f)................. 47
gusto (m).................. **16**
hacer clic 71
hacer una copia de seguridad 71
hacha (m) 37
hamburguesa (f) 24
hámster (m) 75
haya (m) 88
helado (m) 25
helecho (m) 91
hélice (f) 58
helicóptero (m) 59
hermana (f) 10
hermanastra (f) 11
hermanastro (m) 11
hermano (m) 10
herramientas del artista (pl) .**45**
hervidor eléctrico (m)......... 20
hidroavión (m) 59
hidrodeslizador (m)........... 60
hierba de las Pampas (f)....... 91
hierro (m) 65
hígado (m) 15
higos (pl) 26
hilo conductor (m) 63
hipopótamo (m) 72
historia 33

hockey sobre hielo (m)........... 39
hoja (f) 91
hojas (pl) 89
hombro (m) 13
hora (f) **113**
horario (m) 32
hormiga (f) 83
hospital (m) 92
hotel (m) 93
huevos (pl) 23
húmedo.................... 16
iglesia (f) 67
iglú (m) 18
iguana (f) 76
impermeable 65
impresora (f) 70
imprimir 71
ingeniero, ingeniera (m/f)...... 34
inglés 33
iniciar sesión 71
insecto palo (m) 82
insectos y bichos (pl) **82**
insertar 71
instrumentos de cuerda (pl)
   .... **47**
instrumentos de percusión (pl)
   .... **47**
instrumentos de teclado (pl)
   .... **46**
instrumentos de viento (pl)
   .... **46**
instrumentos musicales (pl)
   .... **46**
interior de la Tierra............**104**
interior de un volcán.............**105**
interior de una manzana **27**
interruptor (abierto) (m).......... 63
interruptor (cerrado) (m) 63
intestino (m) 15
intoxicación por pesticidas (f)102
isópodo gigante (m) 80
jabón (m) 21
jazz (m) 48
jefe de cocina, jefa de cocina
   (m/f) 35
judías (pl) 27
juego de mesa (m) 42
juegos y pasatiempos (pl)....... **42**
juguetería (f) 95
Júpiter 106
lagarto (m) 76
lago (m) 99
lámpara (f) 63
lana (f) 64

lancha motora (f) 60
langosta (f)................. 80
langosta mantis (f) 80
lanzar..................... 40
lápiz (m) 33
latón (m) 65
lava líquida (f)...............105
lava sólida (f) 105
lavanda (f) 89
leche (f) 22
lechuza (f) 85
lémur (m) 84
lentejas (pl) 23
león (m) 73
leopardo (m) 72
libélula (f) 83
librería (f) 94
libro de texto (m) 33
limonero (m) 89
limones (pl) 26
limpiaparabrisas (m) 54
linterna sumergible (f) 36
lirio (m) 90
lirón (m)................... 85
liso 65
llama (f)................... 73
llanura (f) 104
llave inglesa (f) 37
llave USB (f) 71
lluvia ácida (f) 103
lluvioso 100
lobo gris (m) 84
loro (m).................... 75
lucio (m) 79
luna (f) 107
macedonia de frutas (f)........... 25
madera (f).................. 64
madre (f)................10, 11
maestro, maestra (m/f) 35
magdalena (f)............... 25
magnético 65
maíz (m).................27, 96
maletero (m) 54
mallas (pl) 28
mamba (f) 77
mamíferos (pl) **72**
manguera (f)................ 37
manivela (f)................ 69
manivela de control (f)...........108
mano (f) 13
manta (f) 78
mantis religiosa (f) 82
manto (m) 104
manzano (m) 89

Índice español • Spanish index

mapache (m) 85
maqueta (f) 42
máquinas sencillas (pl) **69**
maracas (pl) 47
marcar 39
margarita (f) 91
mariposa (f) 83
mariquita (f) 83
Marte 106
martillo (m) 37
martín pescador (m) 86
máscara de buceo (f) 36
mascarilla (f) 36
mástil (m) 60
matemáticas 33
matrícula (f) 54
medias (pl) 29
medicamento (m) 21
medidas (pl) **111**
medusa gigante 80
mejillas (pl) 12
mejor amigo(a) (m/f) 11
melocotones (pl) 26
Mercurio 106
mesa (f) 19
meses (pl) **112**
meseta (f) 104
meteoro (m) 107
mezquita (f) 67
micrófono (m) 50
mimosa (f) 89
minarete (m) 67
mirlo (m) 86
módulo de aterrizaje lunar (m)
.... 109
módulo de control del traje
espacial (m) 108
módulo de mando (m) 108
mofeta (f) 84
momento 68
momentos del día (pl) **112**
monitor (m) 50
mono (m) 72
monopatín (m) 42
montaña (f) 98, 104
montar (a caballo) 41
morsa (f) 80
mosca (f) 82
mosquito (m) 83
moto (f) 54
motocicleta (f) 55
motonieve (f) 57
motoniveladora (f) 56
motor 63

motor a reacción (m) 59
muñeca (f) 13
músculo (m) 14
museo (m) 92
musgo (m) 91
música 33
música clásica (f) 48
música folk (f) 48
música (f) **y baile** (m) **48**
música global (f) 49
naranjas (pl) 27
narciso (m) 90
nariz (f) 12
natación (f) 39
nautilo (m) 80
nave de la maquinaria (f) 97
nenúfar (m) 90
Neptuno 107
neumático (m) 54
noticias (pl) 53
novela (f) 42
nublado 100
núcleo externo líquido (m) 104
núcleo interno sólido (m) 104
números (pl) **110**
océano (m) 98, 105
oficina (f) 92
oficina de correos (f) 94
oído (m) **16**
ojo (m) 12
ojo compuesto (m) 82
ojo de buey (m) 61
óleo (m) 45
olfato (m) **16**
olivo (m) 89
opaco 65
operaciones aritméticas **111**
operaciones en el ordenador (pl)
.... **71**
opérculo (m) 79
opuestos (pl) **115**
ordenador (m) 70
ordenador portátil (m) 71
ordenadores y dispositivos
electrónicos (pl) **70**
oreja (f) 12
órgano (m) 46
órganos (pl) **15**
orgulloso 17
orilla del mar (f) 98
ornitorrinco (m) 73
oro (m) 65
orquídea (f) 90
oruga (f) 83

oso polar (m) 72
oveja (f) 74
padrastro (m) 11
padre (m) 10
paella (f) 24
página inicial (f) 70
pagoda (f) 66
paisaje (m) 44
paisajes y habitáts (pl) **98**
pajarería (f) 95
pájaro carpintero (m) 86
pala (f) 97
pala retroexcavadora (f) 56
palabras de astronomía (pl) ....
....**107**
palabras de posición (f) **115**
palabras de tiempo **112**
palacio (m) 67
palafito (m) 18
palanca (f) 69
palas del rotor (pl) 58
paleta (f) 45
palillos chimos (pl) 20
palloza (f) 18
palmera (f) 88
pan (m) 23
panadería (f) 95
pandereta (f) 47
pangolín (m) 73
pantalla (f) 70
pantalones cortos (pl) 29
pantera (f) 73
papel (m) 64
papelera (f) 94
para hablar de temperaturas (pl)
....**101**
parabrisas (m) 54
parachoques (m) 54
parada de autobús (f) 94
parapeto (m) 66
parking (m) 93
parque de bomberos (m) 92
parquímetro (m) 94
partes de un árbol (pl) **89**
partes de un barco **61**
partes de un coche (pl) **54**
partes de un pez (pl) **79**
partes de una planta en flor (pl)
....**91**
pasar el corrector ortográfico 71
pasta (f) 23
pasta de dientes (f) 21
pastel (m) 45
pastillas (pl) 21

patatas (pl) 23, 27, 96
patatas fritas (pl) 23
patín de aterrizaje (m) 58
patinar 41
patines en línea (pl) 42
pato (m) 75
pavo (m) 75
pavo real (m) 86
peces (pl) **78**
pecho (m) 13
peciolo (m) 91
pedúnculo (m) 27
pegar 71
pelícano (m) 87
película de acción y de
aventuras (f) 52
película de ciencia ficción y
fantasía (f) 52
película de terror (f) 52
pelo (m) 12
peluquería (f) 95
penalti (m) 39
pensamiento (m) 90
pepino (m) 27
pepino de mar (m) 80
pepitas (pl) 27
peras (pl) 27
perezoso (m) 73
periquito (m) 75
perro de rescate de montaña
(m) 75
perro marino (m) 79
perro pastor (m) 74
pescado (m) 23
pétalo (m) 91
petirrojo (m) 86
petróleo (m) 63
pez ángel (m) 79
pez espada (m) 78
pez volador (m) 80
piano (m) 46
pico (m) 97
pie (m) 13
piedra (f) 65
piel (f) 27, 64
pierna (f) 13
pieza de ajedrez (f) 42
pila (f) 63, 67
pimientos (pl) 26
pináculo (m) 66
pincel (m) 45
pingüino (m) 87
pino (m) 88
piraña (f) 79

pivote *(m)* 69
pizarra Vileda® *(f)* 33
pizza *(f)* 24
planeador *(m)* 59
plástico *(m)* 64
plata *(f)* 65
plataforma de lanzamiento *(f)*
.... 108
plátanos *(pl)* 27
platija *(f)* 79
platillos *(pl)* 47
plato principal **24, 25**
platos exóticos **25**
playa *(f)* 105
polea *(f)* 69
polilla *(f)* 82
polilla luna *(f)* 84
pollo *(m)* 24
pomada *(f)* 21
pop *(m)* 48
popa *(f)* 61
porcelana *(f)* 64
portero, portera *(m/f)* 39
póster *(m)* 32
postre *(m)* 23
postres *(pl)* **25**
praderas *(pl)* 98
primos *(pl)* 11
proa *(f)* 61
productor, productora *(m/f)* .. 50
programa concurso *(m)* 53
programa de humor *(m)* 53
programa deportivo *(m)* 53
programas de televisión y
películas *(pl)* **52**
propiedades de los materiales
(pl) 65
público *(m)* 50
pueblos y ciudades *(pl)* **92**
puente colgante *(m)* **67**
puercoespín *(m)* 85
puerta *(f)* 19
pulga *(f)* 83
pulmón *(m)* 15
pulpa *(f)* 27
pulpo *(m)* 80
pulpo dumbo *(m)* 80
punzante 16
pupitre *(m)* 33
quad *(m)* 97
queso *(m)* 23
quimono *(m)* 30
quiosco *(m)* 94
quitanieves *(m)* 57

radiación *(f)* 102
raíz *(f)* 89, 91
rallador *(m)* 20
ramas *(pl)* 89
rana del dardo *(f)* 77
rap *(m)* 49
rápidos *(pl)* 99
raqueta *(f)* 42
raros y extraordinarios *(pl)* **73**
rascacielos *(m)* 67
rastrillo *(m)* 97
ratón *(m)* 70, 75
reciclaje *(m)* 103
redil *(m)* 97
reggae *(m)* 49
región polar *(f)* 99
regla *(f)* 33
reina medieval *(f)* 30
rejilla del radiador *(f)* 54
reloj *(m)* 32
remar 41
repollo *(m)* 27
reportero, reportera *(m/f)* ... 35
reproductor de MP3 *(m)* 71
reproductor de música *(m)* 42
reptiles y anfibios *(pl)* **76**
repugnante 16
restaurante *(m)* 93
retrato *(m)* 44
retrovisor lateral *(m)* 54
reutilización *(f)* 103
revista *(f)* 42
rinoceronte *(m)* 72
riñones *(pl)* 15
riostra *(f)* 59
roble *(m)* 88
robot explorador de Marte *(m)*
.... 109
rock *(m)* 48
rodilla *(f)* 13
romano *(m)* 30
romero *(m)* 89
ropa de diario **28**
rosa *(f)* 90
rótula *(f)* 14
rueda *(f)* 69
rueda y el eje *(f)* **69**
rugby *(m)* 38
sala de estar *(f)* 19
salado 16
salamandra *(f)* 76
salmón *(m)* 79
saltamontes *(m)* 83
saltar 41

sandalias *(pl)* 30
sandía *(f)* 27
sapo *(m)* 77
sardina *(f)* 79
sari *(m)* 31
sarten *(f)* 20
sarten wok *(f)* 20
satélite de comunicaciones .. 109
satélite de observación de
la Tierra 109
satélite meteorológico 109
satélites *(pl)* **109**
Saturno 107
saxofón *(m)* 46
sección del combustible *(f)* 108
secuoya *(f)* 88
selva tropical *(f)* 98
sentidos y sentimientos *(pl)* .. **16**
serpiente de coral *(f)* 77
serpiente de mar *(f)* 80
serpiente pitón *(f)* 77
serpientes *(pl)* **77**
sicomoro *(m)* 89
sierra *(f)* 37
silencioso 16
silla *(f)* 19
símbolos de un circuito eléctrico
(pl) **63**
sinagoga *(f)* 66
sintetizador *(m)* 46
sistema solar *(m)* **106**
sitar *(m)* 47
soja *(f)* 96
Sol *(m)* 106
soleado 100
sombrero de copa *(m)* 31
sonda espacial *(f)* 109
sopa *(m)* 24
sopa de ortigas *(f)* 25
sorprendido 17
soul *(m)* 49
suave 16
subir 70
sudadera *(f)* 28
supermercado *(m)* 93
SUV *(m)* 55
tabla *(f)* 47
tabla de cortar *(f)* 20
tabla de windsurf *(f)* 60
tablero *(m)* 67
tablero de ajedrez *(m)* 42
tablet *(m)* 71
tacto *(m)* **16**
taladro *(m)* 37

tallas *(pl)* 66
tallo *(m)* 91
talón *(m)* 13
tapas *(pl)* 25
tapiz 45
tarántulas fritas *(pl)* 25
tarsero *(m)* 85
tarta *(f)* 25
taxi *(m)* 55
té *(m)* 22
té verde *(m)* 22
teclado *(m)* 70
teclear 71
técnico de sonido *(m)* 50
tecnología 33
tejado *(m)* 19, 66
tejo *(m)* 88
tejón *(m)* 84
teleférico *(m)* 55
teléfono móvil *(m)* 71
telesquí *(m)* 55
televisión *(f)* 19
televisión, cine y teatro **50**
telón *(m)* 50
templo *(m)* 66
tenedor *(m)* 20
tenis *(m)* 38
tertulia *(f)* 53
tetra neón *(m)* 79
tía *(f)* 11
tiburón ballena *(m)* 80
tiburón blanco *(m)* 78
tiburón boreal *(m)* 80
tiempo *(m)* **100**
tienda *(f)* 94
tienda de golosinas *(f)* 95
tienda de periódicos *(f)* 95
tienda de regalos *(f)* 95
tienda de ropa *(f)* 95
Tierra *(f)* **104, 106**
tijereta *(f)* 83
timbre *(m)* 63
timón *(m)* 59
tío *(m)* 11
tipi *(m)* 18
tipos de contaminación *(pl)*
.... **102**
típula *(f)* 82
tirar 40, 68
tirarse de cabeza 40
tiritas *(pl)* 21
tiro con arco *(m)* 38
tiro libre *(m)* 39
tiza *(f)* 45

Índice español • *Spanish index*

tobillo *(m)* 13
todo tipo de comida **24**
todo tipo de materiales **64**
todo tipo de plantas *(pl)* **90**
todo tipo de ropa **30**
todo tipo de tiendas *(pl)* **95**
todo tipo de trabajos **34**
tofu *(m)* 25
toga romana *(f)* 30
tomates *(pl)* 26
tonto 17
topo de nariz estrellada *(m)* 73
topografía del paisaje **104**
tórax *(m)* 83
tormenta *(f)* 101
tornado *(m)* 101
torre *(f)* 67
torre de comunicaciones *(f)* 66
torre de ensilaje *(f)* 97
torreón *(m)* 66
tortilla *(f)* 25
tortuga *(f)* 76
tortuga de mar *(f)* 80
tortuga marina *(f)* 76
trabajo *(m)* 33
trabajos de curso *(pl)* 33
tractor *(m)* 97
traje *(m)* 31
traje de buzo *(m)* 36
traje especial *(m)* 108

traje incombustible *(m)* 37
transbordador espacial *(m)* ... 109
transparente 65
tráquea *(f)* 15
travieso 17
tren *(m)* 55
tren de aterrizaje *(m)* 58
triciclo *(m)* 59
trigo *(m)* 96
triste 17
tritón *(m)* 77
trompeta *(f)* 46
tronco *(m)* 89
trucha *(f)* 79
tulipán *(m)* 90
turbante *(m)* 31
twitear 70
unidad tripulada de maniobra
    (f) 108
Urano 107
uvas *(pl)* 96
vaca *(f)* 75
valle *(m)* 104
vampiro *(m)* 84
vaporera *(f)* 20
vaqueros *(pl)* 28
váter *(m)* 19
vehículo anfibio *(m)* 57
vehículo pesado *(m)* 57
vehículos de pasajeros *(pl)* **54**

vehículos pesados *(pl)* **56**
Vehículos y máquinas agrícolas
    (pl) 97
vejiga *(f)* 15
vela *(f)* 60
velero *(m)* 61
velo de novia *(m)* 31
venda *(f)* 21
vendaval de polvo *(m)* 101
ventana *(f)* 19, 67
Venus 106
verdura *(f)* 23
vertido de petróleo *(m)* 103
vestido *(m)* 28
vestido de novia *(m)* 31
vestuario *(m)* 50
veterinario, veterinaria *(m/f)* ... 34
Vía Láctea *(f)* 107
viajes espaciales *(pl)* **108**
víbora puff *(f)* 77
videoconsola *(f)* 42
vidrio de colores *(m)* 45
violín *(m)* 47
visera *(f)* 37
vista *(f)* 16
vistoso 16
viviendas de distintas partes
    del mundo *(pl)* **18**
volante *(m)* 42
voleibol *(m)* 38

wifi *(m)* 70
wrap *(m)* 24
yate *(m)* 60
yelmo *(m)* 30
yogur *(m)* 23
yoyó *(m)* 42
yudo *(m)* 39
yurta *(f)* 18
zampoña *(f)* 46
zanahorias *(pl)* 26
zapatería *(f)* 95
zapatero *(m)* 82
zapatillas de deporte *(pl)* 28
zapatos *(pl)* 28
zarigüeya *(f)* 85
zona pantanosa *(f)* 99
zorro *(m)* 85
zuecos *(pl)* 31
zuecos de goma *(pl)* 36
zumo de fruta *(m)* 22

Índice inglés · *English index*

abdomen 83
absorbent 65
acid rain 103
action and adventure 52
actor.. 50
air pollution 102
air tank 36
aircraft...................................... **58**
alligator...................................... 77
ambulance 57
amphibians.............................. **76**
amphibious vehicle................... 57
anchor 61
ancient Roman........................... 30
anemone 80
angelfish 79
angry... 17
animal pen.................................. 97
ankle 13
ant 83
antenna 82
aphid... 83
apple... **27**
apple *(tree)* 89
apron 31
archery 38
architect 34
arm.. 13
armadillo 85
Art **33, 44**
artist's equipment **45**
ash... 105
astronaut...................................108
athletics 38
attachment................................. 70
audience 50
aunt... 11
avocados 26
axe... 37
axle.. 69
back... 13
back up.. 71
backhoe loader 56
badger... 84
baker... 95
balcony 67
baler.. 97
ballet... 49
ballroom dancing....................... 49
bamboo 91
bananas....................................... 27
bandage....................................... 21
bank 94
baobab 88

bar 69
bark 89
barn... 97
baseball....................................... 38
basket.. 59
basketball.................................... 39
bat *(animal)* 84
bat *(for games)*....................... 42
bath... 19
bathroom **19, 21**
bathroom cabinet 21
battery 63
beach.. 105
bed 19
bedbug 83
bedroom 19
beech 88
best friend 11
bicycle... 55
bioenergy.................................... 62
biplane 58
birds... **86**
black hole 107
blackbird 86
bladder 15
blog 70
blouse 31
blue marlin 78
blue whale................................... 80
board game 42
boats **60**
body **13**
bonnet 54
bookshop..................................... 94
boom 60
boot *(car)* 54
boots 29
bored... 17
bow *(boat)* 61
bow *(for an instrument)*........... 47
bowl 40
brain.. 15
branch... 89
brass 65
bread... 23
breakdancing.............................. 49
breastbone 14
breastplate 30
breathing apparatus................... 37
bright 16
bronze 65
brother 10
browse... 70
bud 91

budgerigar.................................. 75
builder.. **37**
buildings and structures........ **66**
bulb (light) 63
bulldozer..................................... 56
bumper.. 54
burger 24
bus driver 34
bus station 92
bus stop 94
butcher 95
butterfly 83
buzzer 63
cabbage 27
cable car 55
cactus 91
cafe 94
calculator 33
camel 72
camera 50, 108
camera operator 50
campervan 54
canoe 61
cap...................................... 28, 36
car park 93
car transporter 57
cardigan 28
carrots 26
cartoon 44, 53
carvings 66
castle 66
cat 75
catamaran 61
catch 41
cello... 47
chair 19
chalet.. 18
chalk 45
chameleon 76
charcoal 45
chat 70
cheeks 12
cheese 23
cheetah 73
chef 35
chemist 95
cherries 27
cherry (tree) 89
cherry picker 56
chess pieces 42
chessboard 42
chest 13
chicken 24
chimney 19

chin.. 12
china 64
chipmunk.................................... 73
chips 23
chocolate 23
chopping board.......................... 20
chopsticks................................... 20
church 67
cinema 93
cities... **92**
city hall....................................... 93
clapperboard 50
clarinet 46
classical music 48
click 71
cliff 105
cloak 30
clock 32
clogs 31
clothes **28, 30**
clothes shop 95
cloudy..100
coach 55
coal.. 63
cockerel 75
cockpit 59
cockroach 83
cod 79
coffee... 22
cold..................................... 16, 101
collarbone 14
colourful...................................... 16
colours **114**
column 67
combine harvester...................... 97
comedy 52
command module 108
communications mast............... 66
communications satellite 109
composting 103
computer..................................... 70
computer actions..................... **71**
computers and electronic
  devices.. **70**
confused 17
connect 70, 71
conservation **102, 103**
constellation...............................107
control bar.................................. 58
control handle............................108
convenience store...................... 94
cooker.. 19
cool..101

Índice inglés • English index

copper 65
coral snake 77
core 27
costume 50
cottage 18
cotton 64
cotton wool 21
country 96
coursework 33
cousins 11
cow 75
crane 56
crater 105
cricket 39
crisps 23
crocodile 77
crops and vegetables **96**
crown 30
crust 104
cuckoo 86
cucumber 27
cupcakes 25
curry 24
curtains 50
cut 71
cycling 38
cymbals 47
daddy long legs 82
daffodil 90
daisy 91
dance **48, 49**
dancer 50
dandelion 91
days of the week **112**
deck (boat) 61
deck (bridge) 67
deer 73
defender 39
delete 71
delivery van 57
desert 98
desk 33
dessert 23
dhow 61
digital camera 71
director 50
dive 40
diver **36**
diving mask 36
dogfish 79
dolphin 80
dome 67
donkey 75
door 19

dormouse 85
double-bass 47
download 70
drag 71
dragonfly 83
dress 28
drinks **22**
drums 47
duck 75
duck-billed platypus 73
dull 65
dumbo octopus 80
dumper truck 56
dust storm 101
DVD 42
eagle 87
ear 12
earphones 42
Earth **104, 106**
Earth observation satellite 109
earwig 83
edit 71
eel 78
eggs 23
Egyptian cobra 77
elbow 13
electric drill 37
electrical circuit **63**
elephant 72
email 70
energy and power **62**
energy conservation **103**
energy saving 103
engineer 34
English 33
envelope 59
equator 101
e-reader 71
estate car 54
estuary 99
eucalyptus 89
evergreen forest 98
everyday clothes **28**
exam 33
excited 17
exercise book 33
eye 12
eyebrow 12
face **12**
family and friends **10**
fan 30
farm buildings **97**
farm house 97
farm vehicles and machinery 97

father 10
feelings **16**
fern 91
ferry 60
figs 26
file 33
film **50, 52**
fin 79
fingers 13
fir 88
fire engine 57
fire station 92
firefighter **37**
fireproof boots 37
fireproof suit 37
fish 23, 78
fish **78**
fizzy drink 22
flamingo 87
flea 83
flesh 27
flipper 36
float 58
florist 95
flower 91
flute 46
flying fish 80
foggy 100
folk 48
food **22, 24, 25**
foot 13
football **38, 39, 42**
football boots 29
forces and machines **68**
forehead 12
fork 20
forklift truck 56
format 71
fox 85
fractions **112**
free kick 39
freezing 101
friction 68
fried tarantulas 25
friends 10, 11
frigate bird 87
frogs' legs 25
fruit 23, 26
fruit and vegetables **26**
fruit juice 22
fruit salad 25
frying pan 20
fuel stage 108
fulcrum 69

funicular railway 55
funnel 61
galaxy 107
game show 53
games and leisure **42**
games console 42
garage 19
gateau 25
gauntlet 30
Geography 33
geothermal energy 62
giant isopod 80
giant jellyfish 80
giant squid 80
gift shop 95
gill cover 79
giraffe 72
glacier 98
glass 64
glider 59
globe 33
gloves 29
goal 39
goalkeeper 39
goat 74
going up **55**
gold 65
golf 39
goose 75
gorilla 73
graffiti 45
grandfather 10
grandmother 10
grapes 96
grasshopper 83
grasslands 98
grater 20
gravity 68
great white shark 78
great-grandfather 10
great-grandmother 10
green beans 27
green mamba 77
green tea 22
greengrocer 94
Greenland shark 80
grey wolf 84
guinea pig 75
guitar 47
gymnastics 38
habitats **98**
hailstorm 101
hair 12
hair band 28

Índice inglés • *English index*

hammer 37
hamster 75
hand 13
handle 69
hang-glider 58
happy 17
hard 65
hard hat 37
harp 47
hat 29
hazardous waste 102
head 13, 83
headlight 54
hearing **16**
heart 15
heavy goods vehicle 57
hedgehog 84
heel 13
helicopter 58
helmet 30, 37
helmeted hornbill 87
hen 75
hermit crab 85
heron 86
hill 104
hip 14
hippopotamus 72
History 33
hit 40
holly 89
home page 70
homes around the world **18**
homework 33
honeybee 82
horror 52
horse 74
horse chestnut 88
hose 37
hospital 92
hot 16, 101
hot air balloon 59
hot chocolate 22
hotel 93
housefly 82
household objects **20**
hovercraft 61
hull 58, 61
hummingbird 87
hydroelectric power 62
hydrofoil 60
ice cream 25
ice hockey 39
icy 101
igloo 18

iguana 76
insects and mini-beasts **82**
insert 71
instruments **46, 47**
intestine 15
iron 65
jacket 29, 31
Japanese empress 30
Japanese samurai warrior 30
jazz 48
jeans 28
jet engine 59
jigsaw puzzle 42
judo 39
juggling balls 42
jump 41
Jupiter 106
kangaroo 73
kettle 20
keyboard 70
keyboard instruments **46**
kick 40
kidneys 15
kilt 31
kimono 30
kingfisher 86
kitchen **19, 20**
kite 42
knee 13
kneecap 14
knife 20
koi 79
Komodo dragon 76
ladle 20
ladybird 83
lake 99
lamb 24
landing gear 58
landing skid 58
landscape features **104**
landscapes and habitats **98**
laptop 71
laughing 17
launch pad 108
lavender 89
lawyer 35
leaf 91
leaf stalk 91
leather 64
leaves 89
leg 13
leggings 28
leisure **42**
lemon *(tree)* 89

lemons 26
lemur 84
lentils 23
leopard 72
lessons **33**
lever 69
life support system 108
light pollution 103
lily 90
lion 73
liquid outer core 104
litter bin 94
liver 15
living room 19
lizard 76
llama 73
load 69
lobster 80
log off 71
log on 71
loud 16
lunge 40
lung 15
machinery sheds 97
machines **68, 69**
mackerel 79
magazine 42
magnetic 65
main cable 67
main courses **24, 25**
maize 96
mammals **72**
manned manoeuvring unit 108
manta ray 78
mantis shrimp 80
mantle 104
maracas 47
Mars 106
Mars rover 109
mask 36
mast 60
materials **64, 65**
Maths **33, 111**
measurement **112**
meat 23
meatballs 24
medicine 21
medieval knight 30
medieval queen 30
memory stick 71
Mercury 106
meteor 107
microlight 59
microphone 50

milk 22
milking shed 97
Milky Way 107
mimosa 89
minaret 67
mini-beasts **82**
minnow 79
mischievous 17
mixer truck 57
mobile phone 71
model 42
modelling clay 45
molten lava 105
momentum 68
monitor screen 50
monkey 72
months **112**
moon 107
moon lander 109
moor 99
moped 55
mosque 67
mosquito 83
moss 91
moth 82, 84
mother 10, 11
motor 63
motor boat 60
motorbike 54
mountain 98
mountain-rescue dog 75
mouse *(animal)* 75
mouse *(computer)* 70
mouth 12
MP3 player 71
muscle 14
museum 92
Music 33
music and dance **48**
music player 42
musical instruments **46**
nasty 16
natural gas 63
nature documentary 53
nautilus 80
neck 13
neon tetra 79
Neptune 107
news programme 53
news stand 94
newsagent 95
newt 77
nice 16
nocturnal creatures **84**

Índice inglés • *English index*

noise pollution 102
nose 12
novel 42
nuclear energy 63
number plate 54
numbers **110**
nurse 35
oak... 88
oats 23
ocean...............................98, 105
octopus 80
office 92
oil 63
oil paints 45
oil spill 103
ointment.................................. 21
olive (*tree*)............................. 89
omelette 25
onion.. 26
opaque 65
opposites **115**
oranges 27
orchid....................................... 90
organ 46
organs **15**
ostrich...................................... 87
owl... 85
paddle 41
paella 24
pagoda 66
paintbrush 45
palace 67
palette 45
palm... 88
pampas grass........................... 91
pancakes.................................. 25
pangolin................................... 73
panpipes................................... 46
pansy 90
panther 73
paper 64
parapet.................................... 66
parking meter........................... 94
parrot....................................... 75
parts of a car **54**
parts of a fish **79**
parts of a flowering plant **91**
parts of a ship **61**
passenger jet............................ 59
passenger vehicles **54**
pasta.. 23
paste.. 71
pastels 45
pavement 94

peaches.................................... 26
peacock.................................... 86
pears.. 27
peas 26
pelican 87
pen 33
penalty 39
pencil 33
penguin 87
peppers 26
percussion instruments **47**
pesticide poisoning 102
pet shop 95
petal 91
photograph 44
piano 46
pickaxe 97
pier 67
pike 79
pills 21
pine 88
pips 27
piranha 79
pivot 69
pizza 24
plaice 79
plain 104
planet Earth **104**
plants **90**
plasters 21
plastic 64
plateau...................................104
poison dart frog 77
polar bear 72
polar region 99
police car 57
police officer 35
pollution and conservation..**102**
pond skater 82
pop 48
poppy....................................... 90
porcupine................................. 85
porthole 61
portrait 44
position words......................**115**
possum 85
post box 94
post office 94
potatoes...............23, 27, 96
power **62**
praying mantis 82
print.. 71
printer 70
producer 50

project 33
propeller 58
properties of materials **65**
proud 17
puff adder 77
puffin 87
pull 68
pulley 69
pumpkins..........................26, 96
push 68
python 77
quad bike 97
quiet 16
raccoon 85
racket 42
radiation 102
radiator grille 54
radio mast 67
rainforest 98
rainy 100
rake 97
rap 49
rapids 99
recycling.................................103
redwood 88
referee 39
reggae 49
reporter 35
reptiles and amphibians......... **76**
restaurant................................. 93
re-use 103
rhinoceros 72
ribs 14
rice 23, 96
ride 41
river **99**
road 94
robin 86
rock (*music*)............................ 48
rocket 108
roller 56
rollerblades 42
roof 19, 66
root 89, 91
rope 69
rose 90
roseate spoonbill...................... 87
rosemary 89
rotor blade............................... 58
rough 65
roundhouse 18
rowing boat.............................. 61
rubber 64
rubber (*eraser*)....................... 33

rubber clogs 36
rudder 59
rugby.. 38
ruler 33
sad 17
sail 58, 60
sailboard 60
sailing dinghy 61
salad 25
salamander............................... 76
salmon 79
salty 16
sandals 30
sandwich 24
sardine 79
sari 31
satellite dish 66
satellites **109**
Saturn 107
saucepan 20
save (*computer*) 71
save (*football*)......................... 39
saw... 37
saxophone................................ 46
scales 79
scalpel 36
scan... 71
scared...................................... 17
scarf 29
scenery..................................... 50
school...............................**32, 92**
Science 33
science fiction and fantasy 52
score (*goal*)............................. 39
scorpion 84
screen....................................... 70
screwdriver............................... 37
scroll.. 71
sculpture................................... 45
scythe 97
sea creatures.......................... **80**
sea cucumber........................... 80
sea snake.................................. 80
sea spider 80
sea turtle 80
seahorse 80
seal.. 80
seaplane................................... 58
search 70
seashore 98
seasons................................**112**
senses and feelings................ **16**
shampoo...................................21
shapes..................................**114**

sharp... 16
sheep... 74
sheepdog....................................... 74
shin... 14
shiny.. 65
ships, boats, and other craft ... 60
shirt... 28
shoe shop..................................... 95
shoes.. 28
shoot (sport)............................... 41
shops.. 95
shorts.. 29
shoulder....................................... 13
shower.. 19
shower gel.................................... 21
shrubs... 88
shuttlecock.................................... 42
sieve... 20
sight.. 16
silage tower................................. 97
silly... 17
silver... 65
simple machines.......................... 69
singer... 50
sink... 19
sister.. 10
sitar.. 47
skate... 41
skateboard................................... 42
skeleton.. 14
sketch... 44
sketch pad.................................... 45
ski... 41
ski lift... 55
skin... 27
skip truck...................................... 57
skirt.. 29
skull.. 14
skunk.. 84
skyscraper.................................... 67
sloth... 73
slug... 84
small animals........................ **75**
smell...................................... **16**
smoggy..100
smooth.. 65
snacks..................................... **24**
snakes..................................... **77**
snorkel.. 36
snow plough................................. 57
snowmobile.................................. 57
snowy..100
soap.. 21
socks.. 29

soft..16, 65
solar energy................................. 62
solar system........................ **106**
solid inner core...........................104
solid lava.....................................105
soul... 49
sound engineer............................ 50
soup.. 24
sour.. 16
soybeans....................................... 96
space............................ **107, 108**
space probe.................................109
space shuttle...............................109
space station...............................109
space travel......................... **108**
spacesuit......................................108
spacesuit control module......108
spade.. 97
spaghetti....................................... 25
spanner... 37
spatula.. 20
spell check.................................... 71
spine... 14
sponge.. 21
spoon.. 20
sports...................................... **38**
sports car...................................... 54
sports in action..................... **40**
sports programme......................... 53
spotlight.. 50
squirrel.. 73
stables.. 97
stadium... 93
stage... 50
stage manager............................. 50
stained glass................................. 45
stapler... 33
star..107, 114
star-nosed mole........................... 73
steak... 24
steamer... 20
steel.. 65
stem.......................................27, 91
stepbrother................................... 11
stepfather..................................... 11
stepsister...................................... 11
stern... 61
stick insect.................................... 82
still life... 44
stilt house..................................... 18
sting.. 82
stinging nettle soup...................... 25
stomach...................................13, 15
stone... 65

strawberries................................. 26
stream... 99
street....................................... **94**
street light.................................... 94
striker... 39
stringed instruments............. **47**
strut.. 59
sugar cane.................................... 96
suit... 31
suit of armour............................... 30
Sun..106
sunflower...................................... 90
sunny...100
supermarket................................. 93
surf (Internet).............................. 70
surgeon................................... **36**
surgical gown............................... 36
surprised....................................... 17
suspender cable............................ 67
suspension bridge.................. **67**
SUV... 55
swallow (bird).............................. 86
swamp... 99
sweatshirt..................................... 28
sweet.. 16
sweet shop.................................... 95
sweetcorn..................................... 27
sweets... 23
swimming...................................... 39
switch... 63
swordfish...................................... 78
sycamore...................................... 89
synagogue.................................... 66
synthesizer................................... 46
tabla... 47
table... 19
tablet.. 71
tail fin (aeroplane)....................... 59
tail fin (fish)................................. 79
talk show...................................... 53
tambourine................................... 47
tanker... 60
tap dancing................................... 49
tapas... 25
tapestry... 45
tarsier... 85
taste.. **16**
taxi... 55
tea... 22
teacher... 35
Technology.................................... 33
teeth... 12
television...................................... 19
temperate climate........................101

temperature.......................... **101**
temple... 66
tennis.. 38
tepee... 18
text book....................................... 33
theatre..................................... **50**
thigh... 14
thorax... 83
throw.. 40
thrusters.......................................108
thunderstorm...............................101
tidal energy.................................. 62
tie... 31
tights.. 29
time.............................. **112, 113**
timetable...................................... 32
toad... 77
toes... 13
tofu... 25
toga... 30
toilet... 19
tomatoes....................................... 26
tool belt.. 37
tool tether....................................108
toothbrush..................................... 21
toothpaste..................................... 21
top hat.. 31
tornado...101
tortoise.................................... **76**
touch.. **16**
tower... 67
towns and cities..................... **92**
toy shop.. 95
tracksuit top.................................. 29
tractor... 97
train.. 55
trainers... 28
transparent.................................... 65
trees and shrubs..................... **88**
tributary.. 99
trike... 59
tropical climate.............................101
trout.. 79
trumpet... 46
trunk... 89
T-shirt... 29
tulip.. 90
tuna.. 78
turban... 31
turkey... 75
turret.. 66
turtle... 76
TV shows and films................ **52**
TV, film, and theatre........ **50, 52**

Índice inglés · *English index*

tweet	70	walrus	80
type	71	warm	101
tyre	54	wasp	82
uncle	11	water	22
upload	70	water buffalo	74
Uranus	107	water contamination	102
valley	104	water lily	90
vegetables	23, 26, 96	watercolour landscape	44
vehicles	**54, 56, 97**	watercolours	45
veil	31	waterfall	99
Venus	106	watermelon	27
vet	34	waterproof	65
violin	47	waterproof torch	36
visor	37	wax	64
volcano	**105**	**weather**	**100**
volleyball	38	weather satellite	109
vulture	87	wedding dress	31
waistcoat	31	weight belt	36
wall chart	32	wet	16

wet suit	36	woodland	98
whale shark	80	woodpecker	86
wheat	96	wool	64
wheel	69	**work**	**34**
wheel and axle	**69**	**work equipment and clothing**	**36**
wheelbarrow	97	**working animals**	**75**
whiteboard	33	**working vehicles**	**56**
wi-fi	70	world music	49
wind instruments	**46**	wrap	24
wind power	62	wrist	13
window	19, 67	writing pad	33
windpipe	15	yacht	60
windscreen	54	yew	88
windscreen wiper	54	yoghurt	23
wing	59	yo-yo	42
wing mirror	54	yurt	18
wire	63	zebra	73
wok	20		
wood	64		

OXFORD
UNIVERSITY PRESS

Great Clarendon Street, Oxford OX2 6DP

Oxford University Press is a department of the University of Oxford. It furthers the University's objective of excellence in research, scholarship, and education by publishing worldwide in

Oxford New York Auckland Cape Town Dar es Salaam
Hong Kong Karachi Kuala Lumpur Madrid Melbourne Mexico City Nairobi New Delhi Shanghai Taipei Toronto

With offices in
Argentina Austria Brazil Chile Czech Republic France Greece Guatemala Hungary Italy Japan Poland Portugal Singapore South Korea Switzerland Thailand Turkey Ukraine Vietnam

© Oxford University Press 2013

All artwork by Dynamo Design Ltd.
Cover images: Spanish flag, Globe Trotter, LLC/Shutterstock.com. Magnifying glass, Vjom/Shutterstock.com. All others Dynamo Design Ltd.
Developed with, and English text by, Jane Bingham and White-Thomson Publishing Ltd.
Translated by Carmen Fernández Marsden

British Library Cataloguing in Publication Data available

ISBN: 978 0 19 273373 3

10 9 8 7 6 5 4 3 2 1

Printed in China